EFFECTIVE MANAGEMENT

20 keys

TO A WINNING CULTURE

A. Keith Barnes

ASTD
WORKPLACE LEARNING & PERFORMANCE
PRESS

ASTD Press is an internationally renowned source of insightful and practical information on workplace learning, performance, and professional development.

ASTD Press
1640 King Street Box 1443
Alexandria, VA 22313-1443 USA

Ordering information: Books published by ASTD Press can be purchased by visiting ASTD's website at store.astd.org or by calling 800.628.2783 or 703.683.8100.

Library of Congress Control Number: 2012954030
ISBN-10: 1-56286-858-6
ISBN-13: 978-1-56286-858-1
e-ISBN: 978-1-60728-520-5

ASTD Press Editorial Staff:
Director: Glenn Saltzman
Manager, ASTD Press: Ashley McDonald
Community of Practice Manager, Workforce Development: Ron Lippock
Associate Editor: Heidi Smith
Editorial Assistant: Sarah Cough
Text and Cover Design: Lon Levy
Printed by: Versa Press, East Peoria, IL, www.versapress.com

Table of Contents

Acknowledgments

I must express deeply felt gratitude to all the mentors who influenced my personal and professional growth and development; yes, there have been many. But in particular, I am grateful to my older brother, John— my first personal mentor—and especially Jack Cole, my first workplace mentor. Jack was an incredible tour guide for the journey through life. But the truth is that I learned something of value from almost everyone I have ever known: colleagues, students, friends, and my incomparable and loving wife, Judy.

Special thanks are also due to Steven Hutson, my agent at WordWise Media Services. Steve's patient understanding and careful attention to this and all my written works, and his diligent search for a suitable outlet, are much appreciated.

It is especially rewarding to be associated with the American Society for Training & Development. For decades, the products, services, and programs of ASTD have aided in the development of human talent in an impressive array of situations around the world.

I am grateful for the opportunity to contribute to their efforts.

KB

Foreword

By Greg Horn, MBA

CEO, Essentient Inc., and former CEO of General Nutrition Centers (GNC)

Culture is the single most powerful force in determining the performance of an enterprise. It is what shapes strategy and determines the level of effectiveness in its execution. Culture serves to attract talent to an organization—matching and reinforcing talent that ensures progress in kind—and it fosters the development of the products and services that attract customers. Culture defines "who we are" and "why we do what we do" as an organization, and it is thus the nucleus of branding and the touchstone for all marketing. Culture can also attract (or repel) strategic and capital partners, and underlies the success or failure of those relationships.

Shaping culture and harnessing its power to achieve the desired results in an organization is a crucial function of management at all levels. This aspect of management is more art than science, yet—especially given its importance—there is surprisingly little practical information available on how to actually create and cultivate a winning culture, though much theoretical work has been done.

To illuminate the subject in a succinct and practical way, Dr. Barnes draws from rich experience as both a successful management practitioner and management professor. He developed his management skills as a senior executive at a Fortune 500 industrial corporation, later bringing his real-world perspective to the university classroom, mentoring and inspiring students to advance into productive and rewarding business careers. I am one of those students.

When we first met, I was a 20-year-old business major trying to learn as much as possible before going out into the real world of work. In Professor Barnes, I found a teacher who had not only managed businesses successfully, but—in what was a significant personal economic sacrifice—was also willing to share his knowledge and experience with the next generation of managers. He became one of my most important mentors, and his insights made an indelible impression on me and helped me develop my own approach to leading and managing everything from turnarounds and startups to multibillion-dollar corporations.

With this book, Dr. Barnes provides insights into effective management and directly usable advice on the creation and sustenance of a winning culture. The guidelines and edicts you'll find in his book can help you become a better manager, and his advice and perspective are presented in a format that is immediately usable, easy-to-digest, and can benefit every practicing manager, from department head to CEO. Read it, keep it handy, and refer to it often; it is that good and that useful a resource.

GH

Introduction

In the everyday life of managers, in businesses large and small—and for that matter, in the nonprofit sector—there occur challenges and threats, opportunities visible and obscure, all variously significant in their impact. Much of the time, in all but the rarest of circumstances, the most serious challenges could have been prevented—or, at least, foreseen and dealt with proactively. Of course, opportunities need to be contextualized in order to assess the latent pitfalls and develop lasting improvements. That requires know-how and insight in leaders familiar with their own industry specifics, but it also calls for a system-wide alertness and a commitment to the development of the human organization…**a winning culture**.

These are sweeping statements, I realize, as many might say that "things just happen," but bear with me and you'll see that I am not talking of the need to be prescient, or even unusually smart. What I'm getting at in these pages (and hoping to help you with) is the all-important process of building and maintaining an organization made up of people who are committed, fully in touch with the products and services your business offers, and also the marketplace in its entirety:

the customers, the competitors, the dynamic circumstances, and the industry milieu.

The use of the word "culture" needs some explanation perhaps, as the most common usage refers to people of common heritage, ethnicity, or race. For purposes here, however, I consider "culture" to be the commonalities that exist among people who have shared interests, such as within one organization, or even within one department of an organization. It is easy to see why the men and women who work in a marketing department (as one example) see their world and their collective challenges in significantly different ways from those in say the accounting function. Dealing with those kinds of potential conflict are addressed herein. But the whole organization, in order to function smoothly and effectively, needs to cohere and set aside petty turf wars of the lesser kind. This book shows ways of meeting that objective: building a coherent team that is alive, awake, attuned, and committed...**a winning culture**.

Here you will find directly usable ideas and guidelines, for what I believe are the keys to creating an effective and efficient team of players at every level who will rise to the occasion most of the time. These people will solve problems even before they become dangerously negative, and will be proactive in taking advantage of positive opportunities presented. The results will include growth, improved profits and other measures of efficiency, and the creation of an enjoyable, rewarding culture for all those on board, as well as the delivery of fair and equitable value (goods and services) to your customers or clients.

Much has been written about "stakeholders," and there is little doubt that forward-looking enterprises are keenly aware of all the various parties directly or indirectly involved in or affected by the processes and products of any organization. But the truth is that there are key players on the inside of any team, individuals who set the tone and build the culture—for better or worse. Key players are not just the top managers; but the edicts, guidelines, methods, and suggestions found in these pages are primarily directed at the key players in an organization. Some people may be tempted to label them "leaders," regardless of the title or rank, and they are certainly that, but they are much more…they are the lynchpins to success. At whatever level they exist in your organization, their consistent adherence to the specific recommendations and the general tenets and philosophies of this book will transfer to others under their influence…and **a winning culture** will develop.

I have written this book as a practical guide, not as an academic treatise, and yet all the guidelines are heavily based on real-world experience as well as research and academic theories. All of the content is tempered by my personal experiences in taking on management challenges in organizations large and small, and creating **a winning culture** in some of the most difficult circumstances. Those who wish to read more in the realm of theory, or see reference materials on all the subjects contained herein, can see my prior book, *Management Maturity: Prerequisite to Total Quality Management.*

Most of the chapters in this book are directed at human processes and the various interfaces between people in the workplace. On the more technical aspects of management and leadership—identifying specific steps to be taken, tasks to regiment within your team—I offer a few approaches, methodologies, and systems that will tighten up your operation in the most critical areas. But between the lines of even these technical contents you will find the human factors stressed. Critically so! Management is primarily about people.

Regarding all those decisions managers face on a day-to-day basis that are not directly related to human organization, I certainly acknowledge their existence and yet I affirm the need for effective management approaches on them too. Such decisions may have to do with products and services offered, facilities and locations, supplier problems, union challenges, local regulations and obligations, and a great many other things. But here's the truth: On all such issues, from the management team and even employees who do not supervise other workers, there will be responsive and responsible actions taken in an organization wherein the guidelines and edicts of this book have been followed, making the decision process more effective. I have always advocated the need to build an organizational ethos in which people at every level do not go to their boss with problems, seeking answers. Instead, they go to their boss to report a problem already solved—or at least with a recommended solution to one proactively recognized. Such is **a winning culture**.

In no case have I written more than the basics on each topic covered, and as you read on you will soon learn why. It would be impossible to do more in an accessible book of this sort—after all, it is not a textbook—but also it would contravene my own philosophy of allowing people to adapt ideas and suggestions, blending them into their own circumstances. You have your own abilities to apply these basics in your setting, so use them according to your own experience and understandings, adapting them to serve your organization, your purposes, and your personal goals.

I make no claim that this collection is complete. There are many similar or related topics for managers and supervisors to address, to understand, and to apply to their particular unique circumstances. But I have chosen this set with one thing in mind: applicability to the widest array of settings. These topics certainly apply (or can be adapted) to every organization except perhaps the very smallest—yet many of them can also be of value there!

At the end of most of the chapters you will find a "Day in the Life of…" exercise. Each of these is in the form of a vignette; a scenario that forms part of a continuing story illustrating an emergent problem or two for key individuals in a fictitious organization. Occasionally in these stories there will be evidence of things done well. The problems and the positives are directly related to the chapter content in each case. These will be restricted; they will not address all of the chapter contents. Rather, they will highlight one or two key topics, giving you an opportunity to respond, observe, and record your thoughts and reflections appropriately. You are invited to make notes and suggest ways in which the problems could have been prevented or alleviated, or to identify what was done right. The most evident things should occur to you readily, but dig a little deeper and see what latent evidence you can identify. The author's notes on these same exercises can be found at the end of the book, with expanded descriptions into topics of relevance when necessary.

Chapter 1

Hiring, Interviewing, and Evaluating Performance

I start with these topics simply because they are the ones all managers must do well, but also because I am convinced these processes are the ones most often mishandled by even the best of managers. Not surprisingly, I see these responsibilities among the most important in determining the quality of your organization.

Hiring

When setting out to hire a new person—whether to fill a vacated position or one newly created—it is essential that you articulate exactly what your needs are before taking any steps. If the new hire is to be a replacement, make sure the envisioned responsibilities for the position are not simply a reflection of what was done by the prior person. Start from scratch each time, defining the ideal needs in relation to the system as a whole. This may seem obvious, but even the slightest level of vagueness or uncertainty in defining this will lead to a disappointing outcome. But so will over-reaching! By over-reaching, I mean stipulating qualifications that are not exactly matched to the tasks and responsibilities the new hire will be assigned.

So build a job description for the position, by all means, but be sure to make this mostly about the *role* the person plays in your organization—not so much about the tasks. Job descriptions that are static have some value, and are certainly better than nothing; but instead, get a good sense of the ways in which the person filling the open position will advance the overall objectives of the department involved, and even those of the overall organization. Remember, even the lowest person on the totem pole serves to advance the company mission to some degree. Spell that out in the job description in addition to identifying essential tasks and responsibilities. Emphasize expected outcomes and specific measurable goals.

It is also a good idea, depending on your potential for growth, to think about what this particular position might lead to—for the incumbent. This is a question candidates are entitled to ask you and to get an honest answer about. So be honest with yourself first of all, and be ready to discuss all the potentials. But if it is a position that really has no further advancement, then be honest about that too. You have nothing to gain by being deceptive or by dangling false hopes.

Before attempting to attract outside applicants for a position, give some thought to those people already on the payroll. Is there someone already on board who might fit the bill if given appropriate training? Is there someone you should at least talk to on an exploratory basis? Filling a position from within is—all other things being equal—the most encouraging thing for other employees to see, but there's a catch or two.

If you see one particular inside person who might be ready for promotion to the open position, be specific about what he must do to become the chosen candidate. Convey these observations directly to the candidate, but also to other insiders who might be interested. If a second (or third) insider is not quite ready, then have that person come to you for a discussion of why the chosen one is included in the pool of candidates and he is not, and be specific about what he needs to do to be considered next time around. This is an important step, and one that helps minimize misunderstanding or frustration, so don't overlook it!

Be absolutely clear about the level of compensation you will pay the new person. One of the most common errors employers make is to pay a new hire more than they were previously paying the departing employee (or the one being promoted). If you lose an employee who was dissatisfied with compensation and then find you must pay more to hire a replacement, then you have been asleep at the switch and have been guilty of taking advantage of an employee. Not a great way to build a winning culture!

Ask around among all your people to see if any of them know of someone who might fill your needs. Showing this level of trust fortifies your relationship with them all, and it makes them feel like genuine insiders. But be prepared (after the interviews) to spell out exactly why the person they recommended did not become the selected one.

Similarly, ask your friends outside the company if they know of a person with the training and the credentials you seek. Then, after all these steps have been taken, go to the media or other bases and announce the opening; let the interviews begin.

Interviewing

Interviewing is often botched, and in ways that seem obvious but really aren't. As with everything else in this book, I do not intend to give a full rundown on every aspect of the interviewing process; just those often overlooked steps that can prevent you from building a winning culture. Here's a list of the most important items:

- ❖ Be ready on time for each applicant interview.

- ❖ If you do not have a private office, find a quiet place or go someplace away from others in your organization. Privacy is critical, although you may want to include others in the interviews, especially those who will work with the newly hired person.

- ❖ Be sure you have read the applicant's materials thoroughly and recently (not two weeks prior, when first submitted). Make notes based on the questions that emerge from each applicant's résumé. Each applicant is unique; treat them appropriately as individuals.

❖ Put all calls and interruptions on hold. The applicant has a right to your undivided attention.

❖ Be friendly. This seems obvious, but too many interviewers seem to think being professional means being stiff and formal. So sit on the same side of the desk as the applicant, rather than across from them, and allow a little small talk at first. It puts the applicant at ease.

❖ Ask what the applicant knows about your business or industry, and fill in the missing information for them or correct their misperceptions. They will respond to this sharing in ways that often surprise you. Watch for nonverbal clues as to how they react internally, and share with them all that they need to know in order to decide if they really have an interest in the job. This is their interview of you too, after all!

❖ Repeatedly invite questions and tell them to make notes if they wish, asking all questions at the end of the interview if they prefer, or as they emerge.

❖ Be sure you know all the current hiring taboos: no questions about marital status, family, personal life, and so on, though these may be volunteered by the applicant if you project openness.

❖ Do not play games! Even if you are a trained behavioral scientist, this is no setting for "getting inside the head" of an applicant. Make sure that all questions you ask are ones you need and can use to help decide the applicant's suitability.

❖ Allow plenty of time, commensurate with the level of the job. A management position first interview should not be less than 40 minutes. It can be more than this for second and follow-up interviews, but somewhat less for lower level positions.

❖ Do not attempt to impress the applicant with your own superiority, your depth of knowledge, or the extent of your own success. It is fine to tell of the successes of the organization itself, but always in terms of "we," not "I."

❖ Be specific about compensation, benefits, and workplace standards such as dress codes, hours, vacations, benefits, and so on. But if you'd rather (and if the appropriate resources exist), have an expert from HR deal with these matters.

❖ When you have finished with all of the job-related (skills/credentials/qualifications) questions, make sure the applicant has all their questions answered too, and then close with these two most important items:

» Tell them where the process stands and what will happen next, including when a decision will be made.

» Close by telling the applicant where he stands too—after the interview. Be as honest as you can about the things that impress you and the concerns that you have, and provide an opportunity for a response. As he leaves, thank him for coming in and urge him to call you (or someone you designate by name) with any follow-up questions or concerns.

❖ After the applicant has left you, make your own set of notes on what you liked and what you found lacking. After several interviews, you may not recall all that you should about each applicant.

❖ Important final point: Do not place too much emphasis on your personal reaction to the vague concept of pleasantness. A certain distraction occurs when you take an immediate liking to someone, or feel an immediate affinity with them. It is important to choose primarily on competence, readiness for the job, and overall attitude. "Pleasantness" is a bonus, nothing more. (This point is invalid when hiring someone in a position that requires pleasantness as the main attribute, of course).

Taking all these steps will extend the interview process, certainly, but it will also ensure that a good relationship begins with this first meeting. Remember, you never get a second chance to create a first impression. You want good people on your team, so show them your best side.

Before leaving this topic, one more caveat: If at any time during the interview process it becomes apparent that the applicant has no chance of being selected, then end the interview early and say exactly why. An apology for bringing the person in should accompany an honest statement of what you overlooked in going through the application materials (or what had been left out). No sense prolonging the agony under false pretenses. It happens!

If this person appears likely to be a finalist for the position, develop a plan for checking references soon, while the interview is still fresh in your mind. If others have also interviewed the candidate, get their feedback as soon as possible, and combine their notes with your own.

Employers and employees are in a relationship: one in which each party gets and gives fair value to the other—or should. Let that be your guiding philosophy, and show it right from the first contact!

Performance Evaluations

Every employee, at every level, has a right to be informed as to how they are doing. There is much more to this than simply having a review meeting once a year, however, and there are a great many pitfalls to be avoided if you are to build and sustain a winning culture.

To be brutally honest, I find the whole notion of conducting a formal appraisal meeting—with the requisite forms filled out and signed by both parties—a travesty and an often unproductive exercise. If an organization is functioning well and there is an ongoing open relationship between employees and their supervisors, then no formalized discussion of performance should be necessary. Indeed, it would be redundant.

How can I make that claim?

It's very simple. People deserve (and need) to know how they are doing on an almost continuous basis. Such knowledge and feedback motivates and encourages them and adds to their sense of participation and contribution; vital elements in any winning culture. So you owe it to them to praise their progress, their achievements, and their successes—and to guide them through their failures and their setbacks **on a frequent basis**.

Babysitting? Hardly!

How, then, can these necessary understandings of their ongoing performances develop? And what about raises and promotions? Admonishment or reprimand? Required documentation for a raise, promotion, or a justified termination? All these necessities have become a standard part of an employee's "file," right?

I acknowledge the Western world has become a place in which much is done to cover our rear ends and protect us from wrongful dismissal complaints and other litigation. So files do need to exist, but in a winning culture there are ways to accomplish the necessary while sustaining the desirable.

You will indeed keep a formal file on each employee, and you should add to it frequently, but you should also make certain the employee is fully informed of its contents. Yes, all of its contents, no surprises!

As often as you can, make objective statements to your people—preferably in their setting, not yours—and be specific. Saying things such as "You're doing a great job, Mary," has little value. Instead, pick something specific on which to comment. "I found that letter you wrote to (client) a strong indication of your understanding of the issues, Mary, and it was most effective. Their response was no doubt rewarding for you. Nice job!"

Drop little "thank you" notes on desks, and express gratitude for specific things accomplished in other ways (not for generalities). You should even praise a solid but less than successful effort. Take that opportunity to suggest ways in which better results might have been possible.

At least once every three months, have a face-to-face informal get-together with each person you supervise and summarize all the previously observed and communicated performance recognitions and critiques. Show that these have been entered into the (admittedly needed) personnel file, and—most important—ask if there's anything they wish to enter into that same file. It could be an explanation for a failing or a slip-up, whatever, but there should be an opportunity of this sort made available every time you meet.

If there are tangible goals to be set for an employee, make sure such targets are not beyond reach. As much as possible, have the employee participate in setting her own goals, and be sure to discuss her performance relative to the goals on a regular basis, informally. Adjust goals as circumstances dictate, but make all changes openly— again, with employee participation.

Use group goals when feasible, and have the group do the evaluations of the individuals as well as of the group as a whole. This is a team-building process that really works. No one likes to let his team down.

Remember this: Evaluation of performance is a necessary, useful, and productive exercise. Do it consistently and openly, frequently and honestly. Scrap the once a year nonsense! Finally, allow the employee to evaluate you. Welcome it. Encourage it. Act on it!

A Day in the Life: Introduction

The company in these scenarios is a dealership for the fictitious Demeter Agricultural Equipment Company (DAE) and for several other manufacturers in the agricultural and light industrial machinery manufacturing business. They sell, service, and rent these machines from their three locations: two in Ventura County and one in Santa Barbara County, California. This private company is owned by Gerry Avilla (75 percent) and John Standish (25 percent). They have 52 employees, and Gerry is the CEO/General Manager while John is in charge of sales and rentals in the main location and in the two branches. Their company has been growing slowly over the years, and total revenues run in the range of $8 to $10 million annually. Profitability levels have been slipping during the current economic downturn—and especially of late, as a key salesperson quit and so did the company's office manager/accounting supervisor.

There are 10 sales representatives, 20 service technicians, 11 people who work in the parts department, and the rest of the staff fulfill clerical and administrative functions. The sales personnel all report directly to John Standish, all others (and John himself) report to Gerry Avilla through their immediate supervisors.

A Day in the Life of Gerry and John . . .

John Standish pulled into the driveway of his home, turned off his engine, and sighed heavily. It had been a long day, and it was already after 8:00 p.m. One of his sales representatives had quit a few weeks back, so John had been forced to pick up the slack while doing his own job.

Kelly Standish greeted her husband at the door with a smile and a kiss, and she said, "You look tired, love. Can't you find a new sales rep and get back to your normal routines?"

John grunted, put down his briefcase and said, "I'm interviewing three candidates tomorrow morning, so I'd like to eat dinner off a tray in the den while I go over their files."

"Okay, but there's not much time, John."

John looked puzzled as they walked into the kitchen. "Time for what?" he asked.

"Did you forget? The contractor is coming over with the final plans." Kelly looked at the wall clock and said, "He'll be here in less than 30 minutes."

John himself had set the appointment, and now regretted it. He knew it would take an hour or more to go over the plans for a major landscaping renovation of their property. Planned work included a new swimming pool and the addition of a "granny" apartment on the side of the house.

"Yeah. I did forget. Think I should call him and cancel?"

"You have canceled once already, John. We need to get him started. Your mother's lease is up in three months. She expects to move in here with us by July 30."

"Oh, boy! I'll just have to go into work early in the morning. Where are the kids?"

"They ate already. Well, Kate and I did. She's in her room. Homework. Eddie's over at a friend's house. Oh, Kate said she needed some help with a math assignment. Later, maybe?"

By the time John got to bed that night he was drained. He tossed and turned for hours, and finally got some sleep…but he slept in late despite good intentions. Arriving at the office at 8:30, he was met by his secretary, who said, "John, your first candidate for the sales position has been waiting 15 minutes. You okay? You look wiped."

John found a young man sitting in his office. He stood and shook John's hand. "Good morning, Mr. Standish. Nice to meet you."

John managed a smile, realized he could not recall the candidate's name and said, "Sorry to keep you waiting. Have a seat. Care for some coffee?"

The young man declined.

John said, "Would you give me a moment to refresh my memory by reading over your résumé again…Gabe?" He had pulled the résumés from his briefcase, and spotted the name on the top one of the three. "It'll just take a minute or two. Here, read the job description and this company brochure while I take a few minutes."

"Thanks. No problem. But my name's Jason, not Gabe."

Readers are invited to make notes on the situation described in the "A Day in the Life" box. You will no doubt see many overt problems in this and the other scenarios that follow many of the chapters. The author's own notes are to be found at the end of the book, and you may wish to compare your responses to his. There are really no right or wrong answers, but shoot for identifying as many errors as possible, and also try to find things you would applaud.

Chapter 2

Mentoring and Training

If you ask any successful person if they made it entirely on their own merits without help and guidance from one or more special people— particularly when they were young—you'd find most are willing to acknowledge the role of mentors in their progress.

There may be exceptions, but I have not encountered one. People need guidance to stretch and grow, to develop a sense of progress as they strive to reach their potentials. They need encouragement and support. They need role models and yes, they need genuine mentors.

What is a mentor? The dictionary definition does not do justice to this important concept, describing it merely as "a wise and trusted counselor," so let me specify what mentors must do for their protégés.

A mentor:

- ❖ makes you feel worthwhile by *rewarding achievement* (praise is a form of reward)

- ❖ helps you increasingly become *aware of your strengths*

- ❖ finds ways for you to stretch and *grow through encouragement*

- ❖ *never lets you down*, personally or professionally.

> On the subject of praise—an important form of reward—the first hugely successful nonacademic book on effective management (Hershey and Blanchard's *The One Minute Manager*, 1980) was based entirely on the importance of finding some reason to praise people. These authors recommended finding people doing good work and praising them openly for it. This is an oversimplification, yes, but it's of great value nonetheless. Their little book remains one of the all-time best sellers on management.

The foregoing prescriptions for mentoring present a tall order, right? Yes they do, and yet any one of us can mentor another individual if we start with the right assumptions.

First and foremost, there is no manipulation involved. You must be sincere.

Second, any praise for undeserved achievement will produce negative results and weaken the potential benefits that might accrue from well-deserved praise.

Third, do not expect miracles. Depending on the personalities of both parties, guidance can be accepted fully or rejected, especially at first—until trust is built. But guidance efforts can also be misinterpreted, so (as with all relationships) allow the trust to build slowly.

Fourth, allow the mentoring relationship to fail if it goes nowhere. Walk away and let someone else give it a try (see chapter 6 on dealing with underperformers).

If you are in a leadership role in your organization, you must be willing to mentor others—but do not push it on an unwilling protégé. Similarly, seek mentoring yourself from those with more experience than you, but only if there is apparent willingness on their part.

Interdependencies exist in all human situations. Functional interdependencies of people working together for common purposes are not the only ones that have significance, however. Those of a more personal nature are also critical. The experienced worker must share their learning with those less seasoned, and this can be done openly and effectively even without genuine mentoring taking place; it happens routinely in all but the most dysfunctional settings. But mentoring carries this process several steps further. Mentoring ensures the maximum benefit for the protégé, but it also engenders a culture that is open, organic, and vibrant (see chapter 11 on mismatches for more on this).

Training—different from mentoring—is equally critical to developing your people and to ensuring their continued growth. Not every individual desires to take on more and more responsibility—and that is natural enough—but virtually everyone wants to become more proficient at what they do. It is one way of ensuring job security, for one thing, and increasing earnings for another, but it also has an even more profound benefit: It instills a sense of fulfillment.

Technical training that people need to do their jobs is often done well, I find; but all too often the trainers forget one vital thing about learning—it takes place inside the learner's brain.

I tell my students that they can learn nothing *from* me. I mean it! No, I do not consider myself a poor teacher, but I do know how people learn. It is a process the learner goes through *internally*. It is how information is processed by the learner that determines the efficacy of the learning process. Two students hear the same lecture. One listens and hears but is passive. The other listens, challenges what he hears or blends it with what he already knows, reflects on it, and compares it with related or similar information. Perhaps he allows the new information to replace the old—or he decides to think on it more—but he is actively involved in a process of discovery, of growth and enlightenment, of *change*. It is the trainer's job to facilitate change: to be a change agent, in fact.

Some kinds of training require specific outcomes. A certain thing should be done in a specific way. For example, if you are training to be an airline pilot there are many specific steps to be taken for safety—if nothing else—and in a specific sequence. But mostly training *merely desires a certain outcome, the specific methods and steps being less critical.* So concentrate on desired outcomes and if someone asks why something must be done a certain way, make sure your answer is not "because I say so," or worse, "because that is always the way we have done it." There is nothing more soul-destroying than bureaucratic nonsense, and it leads to demoralization.

People who invent their own methods for reaching a desirable outcome tend to be more enthusiastic about their job than those given no flexibility, but make sure there is an appropriate match between an individual's ability and preparation (see chapter 10 for more on this subject).

Illustration

This true story illustrates my point on the current topic. I was in a middle-management position, years ago, and I often worked late. Almost every evening as I was leaving, I would say goodnight to the cleaning crew, who worked through the night. Old Joe, an amiable fellow, supervised the cleaners and always had a cheery word. I noticed that he applied wax to the terrazzo floor of our lobby every day. I asked him if it was really necessary to wax that floor so often.

"Sure is, Mr. B.," he said. "The floor wax we use just don't hold up well, and too many people scuff their feet as they pass through here during the day."

"You'd think there would be a product that would stand up better," I said. (This was in the days before advanced polymers.)

"Oh, there is," Joe said. "But it's too expensive. The boss man says we have to use this stuff. Looks good when I'm done, though, don't it? So not my problem."

If Joe knew there were better products, and if a better product led to less frequent waxing, wouldn't it be worth trying? Maybe the overall expense would actually decrease? I said nothing of these thoughts to Joe and left him with a kind word.

The next day I spoke to our controller (he oversaw the cleaning crew) and I told him of my exchange with Joe. "Why not let Joe have the freedom to choose his materials and judge the results on an overall basis?" I said. "First cost isn't everything, as you well know."

A few days later I ran into Joe in a hardware store. We exchanged a few pleasantries and he asked, "Did you say something to Mr. Sanders, about my terrazzo floor?"

"No, why?"

"Well, the damnedest thing. He told me to find a better product, said I would be free to use whatever I thought best, and he gave me an annual budget. Not just for floor wax, but for all our cleaning materials. I believe I can save the company some money and get better results. What do you think of that, Mr. B.?"

"Just great," I said. "But just be sure that floor looks good all the time, Joe."

"Oh, I will. I'm in here checking out all kinds of things that'll make our jobs easier and get better results." He paused, looking pensive. "You sure you didn't say something?"

Joe had been given some freedoms. He now felt more like one of the team.

Though the benefits of delegation are illustrated in the above true story, here is an important caution: Do not deal with this on a piecemeal basis. At every level, and in every function, personnel need to feel the encouragement and inclusion that Joe felt. The importance of a winning culture is in the shared, even-handed approaches that exist throughout. Treat the whole as a team! Each member of the team has a different role to play, but each must feel as though her contribution is vital to goal attainment of the whole. This culture must be evident and pervasive! (But see chapter 19 on the subject of maturity, and chapter 10 on the subject of matchups.)

As for training of the other kind—aimed at improving personal interaction with customers and other employees, or having to do with nontechnical issues—the right approach is to have the best performers do the training on the job, day to day, rather than in a formal setting. This is not to say that a classroom session or two is out of the question, but frankly, hands-on, on-site job training is far superior to any other. And it's ideal in most circumstances. But watch out for personality clashes and the possibility of a domineering individual ruining the learning process. Mature people can deal with pompous and heavy-handed trainers up to a point. But choose your trainers wisely. They can make or break the learning process in all kinds of quirky ways.

Finally, before the next topic, let me say that education and training are very different things. And yet they are too often confused and abused. Training aims at modifying and shaping specific behaviors, whereas education primarily focuses on overall growth, and changing *understanding*, which can then result in many self-initiated changes in behavior.

Set specific standards for your training objectives. If you want regimented performances from people, make certain you know why that is critical. If, however, varied approaches are acceptable in your situation, then focus on outcomes training or even on education, which induces involvement and commitment.

Training is the patterning of individual behaviors of a certain kind, whereas *education* is a process of growth that leads individuals to develop their own understandings and apply such individually to their work and to every aspect of their lives. Many jobs require people who are trained and educated. Be sure you understand these aspects thoroughly. Apply them logically and fairly.

A Day in the Life of Gerry and John . . .

Several days passed, and a new sales representative had been hired. John and Gerry were discussing their current challenges over coffee in Gerry's office. Topics varied from the trivial (like a leaky roof in the parts area, causing some products to be damaged), to the more serious issue of the still-needed new office manager. Several applicants had been interviewed for the critical post, but all seemed to lack the necessary experience in this particular industry.

"I liked that guy, what's his name…Henderson?" John said.

"Yeah. His experience is close, so I could train him, but he seemed abrasive to me. Know what I mean? We have a congenial office, and I don't want to upset people."

John grunted an assent, and said: "Speaking of training, my new sales guy needs training badly; I get the feeling he's been used to having more freedom to manage his own activities than I am comfortable with. As you know, I run a pretty tight ship, and I want to see sales call reports each day, and expense reports no later than Monday morning each week. And he's starting to irritate me with his little hints about needing more freedom, like 'Selling is an individual sport, Johnny.' Calls me 'Johnny' all the time. Sounds like my mother!"

"Just tell him to stop. I had a boss once who called me 'Gerry-Boy.' Had to cut him off at the knees." Gerry laughed. "Has he spent any time with Sergio yet?"

Sergio Talbot was their longest serving sales rep. He had his own quirks, but he was a reliable and reasonably productive salesman who knew the product line better than anyone. He also had a history of adhering perfectly to all of John's required procedures and the bureaucratic formalities of the job. His sales levels were modest, but everyone liked him.

"I really don't want Sergio training him, Gerry. Sergio and I have had a few spats lately, mostly over his call reports but there are other things. As you know, I made it easy by accepting reports twice a week. They all have a laptop or a notebook, you know, but I suspect Sergio is not using his to communicate. He might be moonlighting or something. Not sure what he's up to, but at this stage of the game I'm not convinced he's as committed as he once was. As you know, his numbers are down."

"Yes, I know they are. Any other problems with him?"

"Well, yeah. He gripes about me not showing enough encouragement and appreciation."

"What did you say to that?"

"I reminded him his numbers are down. He's an old pro, Gerry; shouldn't need to be treated with kid gloves. He's made good money with us over the years; a couple of times more than me! His annual performance review is coming up, so I'll get things straight with him."

Gerry grunted. "Listen, John, I have another candidate coming in any minute. You available to meet with her after I'm done? On paper she looks promising."

"Do I have to, Gerry? I'm kinda busy, and you know more about the needs in administration than I do."

"It wouldn't hurt to get a second opinion, John."

"All right…give me a buzz when you're done."

Chapter 3

Meeting Dos and Don'ts

The business world—and that of the nonprofit as well—seems enamored with meetings. I have tried very hard to figure out why this is, and failed. It may just be that we are destined to be stuck with fixed periodic meetings (sometimes even daily) in which we…what? Repeat what we did in prior meetings? All too often this is true!

Don't get me wrong. There are occasions (I'll identify the criteria, below) when a gathering of people for a specific purpose is efficacious. So go ahead and hold meetings when necessary, but be sure you do not make such gatherings a waste of time, or counterproductive. Let me explain.

If there's an important change of some kind about to take place—some new procedure, a new product announcement, or something on that level of significance—then a gathering might be justified and can produce results that are positive (a morale boost or a rejuvenation of some sort).

If there's a blanket need for everyone on a team to be updated or trained on some technicality or procedure, and if bringing everyone together is more cost-effective than communicating the necessary information one-on-one, then hold that meeting.

If there's a need to have all meeting participants brainstorm solutions to emergent problems—in other words, if *you* need collective and organic input that can only come in a gathering—then hold that meeting. Although, with the computer-based services readily available today, such as gotomeeting.com, it is possible to achieve desirable results without wasting direct and indirect costs associated with bringing people physically together.

Other than these circumstances, holding collective meetings too often is merely the manifestation of some manager's need to flex his muscles. But if a meeting is necessary—and I admit there are times—then here's a list of admonishments:

❖ Be honest about why you're calling the meeting. If you cannot lucidly write down some powerful reasons for that gathering—and detail what you expect to achieve—then don't do it!

❖ Develop a written agenda and circulate it in advance to all participants, as early as possible. Don't tease people with vague or misleading hints at something special on the agenda. This will merely start potentially damaging rumors.

❖ If the purpose of the planned meeting is to go over "old" ground, in any way repeating what has been done before, spell out in the agenda why there's a need for a repeat. If just a few people are off the rails in some way, don't call everyone in just to get those few retrained. Handle the prodigals separately, preferably one-on-one (see chapter 6 for more on this).

❖ Invite input ahead of time on meeting topics from everyone involved. Participants in a meeting like to feel that their observations, concerns, needs, and recommendations are aired and heeded. This is perhaps the surest way to see benefit from any meeting. Being brought in to a meeting to be lectured is boring and degrading. Get different people to lead a discussion for example, and rotate that responsibility.

❖ Another tactic that has been used to spice up meetings takes place after the meeting is over, as in taking time out for "play" together. This is not a bad idea, necessarily, but it seldom achieves a lasting boost in morale. It can also be seen as gimmicky.

❖ Celebrations of success and the sharing of success stories can be a great morale booster, so find a success story for *every* get-together you have. Make it genuine! For really big success stories, hold a meeting with just that one item on the agenda.

❖ Never use a meeting to expose the weaknesses of an individual or a department, and especially not to embarrass an employee or a group in any way.

I once had a boss who held meetings to humiliate people in front of their peers. It was soon quite evident that he didn't have the courage or the skill to confront an employee who was falling short, so he used the collective to fortify his positional power base. A fatal flaw of leadership!

This same terrible manager would send collections of paperwork on a subject that he wanted to talk about with one of his people. There would always be a sticky note attached, saying "Can I see you about this?" So people would go to his office. After receiving the first few of these, I sent one package back with another sticky note saying simply, "Yes." That brought the problem to a head, and after a brief conversation with him he ditched this practice in favor of the more personal visit to my office. Much preferred, as it removed him from his territorial temple of power.

These are the most significant guidelines with respect to meetings. Individual circumstances will dictate a departure from the general tenets shown here, of course. But try to adhere to the notion that *a meeting belongs to everyone in attendance*. Just because you are the boss, or perhaps the trainer, doesn't mean a meeting is yours and yours alone. Genuine leaders—and certainly those who develop a winning culture—share decision making of every kind. It does not diminish your power; in fact, it enhances it.

A Day in the Life of Gerry and John . . .

John Standish was planning a sales meeting. In order to try something different, he had persuaded his boss, Gerry, to let him spend money on a guest speaker. He had contacted the nearby state university, to see if any of the business professors were available, but after interviewing two of them, he decided he'd be better off with someone less academic and more motivational. He'd found such a man through a speaker's bureau, and was on the phone with him, seeking information about the man's approach and style.

"So you're convinced that all salespeople need to be 'on-the-ball,' as you put it, with frequent pep talks, lots of pressure and finite attainable goals, and with lavish praise when they meet those goals. That about it? I'm reading from the brochure you sent me."

"Absolutely, Mr. Standish. I can assure you that my pep talk about being self-motivated will get them to a high level—a fever pitch—and then I'll coach you, privately, on how to keep them operating at that same level. It's a simple formula, and one that works well. I guarantee it!"

"A guarantee? So if we don't see an improvement in sales, you'll give us back the money we pay you?"

"Well, yes, provided you can prove to me you have followed all my advice closely and consistently. And after you have given the program some time, say a year or two. But I'd be willing to come back in for a second go-round, too. Sometimes that's necessary."

"For an extra fee, no doubt?"

"Ah, yes. But it will pay for itself, you'll see."

"I'll give it some thought and get back to you."

"My calendar fills up fast, Mr. Standish. No time like the present."

"I said I'd get back to you."

John hung up the phone and muttered, mocking, "No time like the present, Mr. Standish." He instead decided he would conduct the motivational part of the meeting himself. He drafted a list of all the things he wanted covered and printed up an agenda, satisfied that a heavy emphasis on his sales call reports was the key item. It enabled his control of the sales process and allowed for a meaningful performance appraisal.

As John was waiting for the printout, Sergio Talbot stuck his head in the door and said, "You wanted to see me, John?"

"What? Oh, yes, Serge. I didn't see a sales call report for all of last week. What happened?"

Sergio came inside and sat down across the desk from his boss. He sighed heavily and said, "You know, John, I have worked here for 16 years. My sales speak for themselves. I am not a paper pusher, and I don't really like computers, can't seem to get along with mine at all. I spent hours on the thing on Sunday night, trying to send you some information on a competitor's latest incentive program. I thought it had been sent successfully, but later I found out that it had bounced back to me with a message saying 'undeliverable.' A system error, it said. Can't you just let me sell, John, and I'll tell you everything worth knowing by phone or when I come into the office?"

"Sergio, I need everyone to cooperate with my system. Including you, my friend."

Chapter 4

Office Relationships

People working together form friendships, and they also develop negative feelings toward others they have to interact with. These feelings are natural. While such relationships pose problems, they are not nearly so difficult to deal with as long as you remember some basic edicts.

As a supervisor, it is natural for you to want to spend time with those team members whose company you enjoy the most. It may be that you share a common interest—in a sport perhaps, or a political persuasion. Or perhaps it is merely unexplained chemistry, you just feel closer for undefined reasons. Okay, so where's the problem in this?

You must remember that your interactions with others you lead are observable. If you are seen going out for lunch more often with one or two people than with others, or even if you are spending significant blocks of time together in the office, this will be seen by others as evidence of favoritism.

The next time a promotion comes up (and you promote one of your "favorites," even for valid reasons) she is doomed to be seen as undeserving. You, too, will be seen as an unfair manager. These are not the dynamics that lead to a winning culture!

Illustration

There's an old adage that overstates the problem inherent in the scenario I have described, but I mention it here simply to make you aware of the problems in being seen as biased: *The military leader is urged to treat every man under his command with the same level of contempt.* Then, should one soldier decide to shoot him in the back he will have to fight others for that right. This is just one cynical interpretation, of course, and totally inappropriate in a civilian setting (or in the military) but you get the message: No one person should be seen as having privileged access.

By all means, go to lunch with your people—or a ball game perhaps—but spread that privilege around. Not only do such shared personal interactions give the impression of fairness, they also give you an opportunity to learn a great deal about what's going on. The feedback you receive—and the useful information you will derive from listening in those circumstances—is priceless. A winning culture comes when all participants feel as though they are significant, and they will find ways to contribute. Your maturity in this is critical, and you must learn to deal with the inevitable attempts to curry favor by those less mature. Help everyone grow!

So spend *more* time with those who need your attention the most! You are naturally tempted to spend time with the winners on your team more than with the others, but don't. Help those who need help the most, and follow the Chinese proverb:

If you want to be happy for an hour, take a nap.

If you want to be happy for a day, go fishing.

If you want to be happy for a year, inherit money.

To be happy for a lifetime, help someone succeed.

The true leader must see one of her main responsibilities as helping others succeed. Not everyone will respond equally, but enough will respond appropriately to ensure a winning culture develops, and your satisfaction will be multiplied greatly. So will your own success!

A Day in the Life of Gerry and John . . .

Gerry Avilla had been given a pair of tickets for an upcoming Los Angeles Kings hockey game against the Detroit Redwings. He loved hockey, but his wife didn't enjoy sports of any kind. He opened his office door and leaned out. Spotting Jake Lofthouse (his credit and collections man) sitting at his desk, Gerry yelled, "Hey, Jake. What are you doing Saturday night? I have a pair of Kings tickets. Wanna go to dinner and the game?"

Jake grinned and said, "Oh yeah! Wings, right?"

Jake was a real hockey fan, had played minor league in his 20s, but had to quit with bum knees. But Gerry also enjoyed Jake's company; in fact they would often go to the Kiwanis Club lunches together.

"Yes. Should be a great game, unlike last time. Remember? What a blowout! And this time you can drive. Pick me up at the house about 4:30."

Most of the others in the office overheard this exchange, and two of the clerical people exchanged knowing looks, eyebrows raised. Mari Soderling said to her friend Clara, sitting not far away in the open office: "Wanna go get some coffee?" There was a small room in the building set aside for customers and employees to sit and enjoy coffee and other refreshments.

No one else was in the coffee room, so Mari closed the door behind them and said, "Does Gerry ever ask anyone else out for dinner and a game?" She was relatively new, had not been on board for more than a few months. Jake Lofthouse was her supervisor. She added, "That's the second time just since I came here."

"Yeah, well, Gerry is the boss, and he likes Jake a lot. So I guess he can do whatever he wants. He takes John sometimes, but mostly Jake gets the nod. I wouldn't want to go to a hockey game anyway, would you? By the way, their wives go out together sometimes, shopping and such… who knows what else." Clara giggled.

"What are you suggesting?"

"Oh, nothing. But no, I wouldn't enjoy a hockey game. Football, maybe. Want some sugar for your tea?"

"Somebody said Gerry does pay for a company picnic in the summertime, right?"

"Yes. Usually around July 4th weekend. They are fun. Gerry pays for everything, but he doesn't hang around too long. Makes his little speech and then leaves. His wife doesn't even come…well, she did one time. Seems snooty. Drives a Mercedes just like Gerry's. They live up on Saffron Heights, you know."

"Yes, somebody told me. Must be nice!"

Chapter 5

Who Gets the Credit?

In a remarkable book about Ronald Reagan, *A Different Drummer*, written by his longtime friend and associate Michael K. Deaver, I found many great sayings. Reagan had a treasury of them! This is one of his best: "You'd be amazed what can be accomplished if you don't mind who gets the credit."

If you can inculcate this sentiment in your team, by showing it to be part of your own everyday philosophy, you will see remarkable results in a very short period of time. Again, it calls for a level of maturity on the part of everyone, and it also calls for you to be ready to deal almost paternally with pettiness—in the beginning especially— but such setbacks will soon fade and your team will grow immensely.

Recognize individual accomplishments by all means, but no one individual can make a team. It is the collective effort that counts most in the long haul. The quarterback makes a great throw, the receiver a stunning catch, but the blocking and tackling and the preparation by everyone is what makes the great play even possible.

Illustration

I used to teach an undergraduate business policy class in which students worked on assignments outside the class in groups of four or five. The purpose was to teach the value of teamwork, but also to have them realize just how difficult it is to share the outcomes (grades) of a collective effort. Everyone in the group would get the same grade from me, even though I knew that each group had individuals who were brighter, more industrious, or perhaps even more efficient than the others. Such is life.

Midway through the semester, one of those brighter students came to me privately and said how difficult it was for him because he didn't feel his teammates were all contributing as much as he was. I smiled. "Welcome to the world," I said. It is your job to build that team or deal with it appropriately (there was a written provision for "firing" a team member after going through a set of delineated procedures, including my involvement, to ensure fairness.) The student went back to work and I heard nothing more on the subject. My message to him was clear, and it was one I hoped would serve him well in his career. Some years later he conveyed to me that it had, and he thanked me even though his predicament in my class had cost him a few grade points.

This is the shortest chapter in the book, with good reason. Anything else I might say on this subject could detract from the power of this one key to a winning culture: "There's no **I** in team." Apply this one vigorously and consistently!

A Day in the Life of Gerry and John . . .

"What a day!" Gerry Avilla slumped down in his large office chair and reached into his desk drawer for the bottle of bourbon he kept there. He was not a heavy drinker, but would occasionally share a drink in the office—after hours—with John Standish. Usually, such imbibing was to celebrate an achievement of some sort. Today, as far as Gerry was concerned, there was little to celebrate.

Standish accepted the paper cup, half-filled with whiskey, sipped from it and said, "How did the meeting go?" Gerry had been to the headquarters of one of their suppliers, seeking an extension of their floor-plan credit line. Evidently his quest had been unsuccessful.

"Not good," he said. "And then my flight home was delayed for an hour…crappy day! How about you? You got anything good to tell me?"

John Standish had actually been smiling as his boss complained. Now, he grinned broadly and said, "I got the Martinez deal, Gerry."

Gerry seemed dumbfounded. "You're kidding me! How many units?"

"Five DAE-735s. And they want two more on a rental deal for the whole summer. I just knew I could get it done well, there were doubts last week when Lance said Roberto Martinez wanted to go another way, but I managed to change his mind."

"Wow! That'll be more than 200 grand! Big paycheck coming for Lance! When do we have to deliver? We have only one new unit in stock."

"The factory can get the others here by the end of the month. I am stoked, Gerry! Cheers!"

Gerry stood up and reached over the desk to congratulate his sales manager with a handshake, and they touched their cups together in a casual toast. "Lance is doing okay, isn't he, John? Good for him! I like that kid."

"Lance didn't have much to do with it, really. He has kept a close watch on the deal though, I'll give him that much. I'm just glad I stepped into it when I did. Bingo!"

"Yeah, well that sure takes the salt out of my wounds, John. Well done. Can I fill your cup?"

"Oh, yes. Let's enjoy the moment. Best deal I've made so far this year."

"Great. Let's drink to that and many more like it!"

Chapter 6

Dealing With Underperformers

In my own experience, and from what I have gathered from clients, colleagues, students, and friends, dealing successfully with those who don't quite measure up to the standards you expect is one of the greatest challenges a manager can face.

One of the reasons for this is that, in a way, a poor performance shows that *you* have personally failed in some sense. Perhaps you hired or promoted this failing person, and you expected more; or your efforts to bring about change in the errant party have fallen short. Even if you inherited the employee, you have a natural tendency to question whether or not you have done enough of the right things to bring about better results. So self-recrimination is natural, but dispel it immediately. Such sentiments are never productive!

Even if you are to blame—perhaps especially if you are—your responsibility is to come to a conclusion on what can be done about the problem and bring about appropriate change. Firing the errant party and rehiring and training someone new is expensive and should be seen as the last resort unless there is malfeasance on some level, as well as poor performance.

First of all, try to assess—with help from other members of the employee's team, where there are such—whether the problem is one of motivation. A person not motivated to do well is a rotten apple in any barrel and must be dealt with effectively. This does not necessarily mean termination, as first you must determine if there are mitigating factors inherent in the assignment itself or in the environment: conditions of the workplace, other employee interactions, insufficient training, or other similar things.

The personal circumstances an employee is experiencing can be hugely important in their motivation, naturally. Should you concern yourself with such personal issues?

Yes, but only up to a point.

Make a direct approach to the person in question. If you have been handling the appraisal process effectively, as described in chapter 1, then there should be no surprises in this confrontation. Urge him to be honest about whatever is at play in his personal life and in the workplace. Ask if you are correct in your assessment that it is a motivational problem. If not, perhaps an alternative explanation will be forthcoming.

Again, if your ongoing evaluation program has been handled correctly, the errant employee will know of your dissatisfaction. They will also have been given specific and detailed steps to take and will have objectives set for improvement.

It should go without saying that compensation incompatibilities should have been dealt with as an ongoing basic aspect of your role as a manager, but if the issue of money comes out for the first time, openly discuss the matter, but make only those commitments and promises you feel are just and justified. *Increases in pay should be given as rewards for doing well, never for stimulating an improvement!*

Also, be absolutely certain the pay levels of similar workers are not suddenly made disadvantageous by any change you make…especially if you end up giving a raise to an underperformer! Everyone will see that as a boneheaded move, and they will find out.

Ask the underachieving employee if he feels fully competent in his assigned tasks. Ask if additional training would help in that regard. Offer help with outside courses (where appropriate) if that seems to be indicated, or more in-house training as may be justified.

Set a definite timeframe for further discussions, and be specific about what criteria will be used in determining the next move by you. Ask the employee to agree on all next moves, including the possibility of termination.

Many large employers have in-house employee assistance programs to help with such potentially damaging personal problems as substance abuse, mental health issues, sleep deprivation, physical and emotional abuse at home, and other intensely personal matters. Make sure all your employees know of these benefits and, in the case of an underperformer, encourage them to seek help and guidance.

For smaller organizations, there are programs available under the auspices of county or state health departments (some states) as well as through private agencies and other entities. Take the time to find out as much as you can about these services in any event (during times when they are not needed). In an increasingly complicated world, such things are becoming commonplace. Use all such services as you see fit, and with one objective in mind: the overall systemic welfare of your entire team, and the sustenance of a winning culture. A bad performer can do a great deal of harm to these ideals, so act on problems expeditiously but with reasoned compassion.

Sometimes, the failure of one person to measure up can be dealt with effectively by making sure that goals are group set and group evaluated. Then there will be greater likelihood that a resolution will develop organically from within the group.

In chapter 1, I decried the often necessary but bureaucratic requirement of building a file on each employee. While the dominant reason for such documentation is so that you can use it for an open dialog about progress made by each individual on your team, there is the more insidious reason: to prove that you have given a fair and reasonable set of objectives to an employee. Without such, consistently and fairly handled, your position is tenuous at best—especially when faced with a wrongful dismissal suit. This has become a litigious society, so be as thorough and as professional as you can, and make sure that there is not more focus (negative or positive) on any one employee over another. And do not use your files as clubs, or as the bases of threats—but this should be obvious. Remember the old saying: *If you really have power, you seldom need to use it!*

Illustration

I was once transferred to a profit center as general manager, in a multi-location organization where the chief accountant of one of my branches (I was told) was doing a great job. The evidence for this evaluation was in her personnel file. She had been given nothing but strong performance evaluations for the three years she had been in the position. My predecessor had also given her raises based on those evaluations, and she was near the top of the pay scale for her job category. Oh, dear! I soon found that she was not at all worthy of the praise or the salary level. The evidence was concrete and frequent costly errors were made. How the devil does one handle this kind of incompetence, given the previous string of glowing appraisals?

(By the way, this illustrates the problems inherent in mishandling personnel appraisals as well as how to deal with underperformers.)

My choices were few at that point. Fortunately, the person in question had direct reporting responsibility to my administrative officer, with whom I spent a great deal of time discussing an appropriate approach before inviting the errant person in for a discussion. It is always a good idea to have at least two people involved in situations such as this, and the first thing we wanted to know was if she was aware of her errors and the significance of them in the larger context. She did, she said, and apologized, and she assured us that she would pay closer attention. The unfortunate fact is that she was not properly trained or educated for the position; the errors she had been making were related to that shortcoming. But she had, nevertheless, been promoted and praised frequently.

At the end of that first meeting, I asked the woman, a branch accountant, if she felt she needed additional training. She said she realized she did not have the ideal preparation, but felt that her on-the-job learning had prepared her well enough, and she had been assured by my predecessor that she was doing a good job.

To make a long story short (it took two years to resolve), we pressed for the woman to disclose any personal circumstances that would explain her problematical lapses, and she assured us there were none. We offered to pay for additional training and education that would enhance her abilities, and she declined. We finally gave her a timeline for improvement, as well as specific criteria that would be used to evaluate her performance, and she agreed to them with reluctance. After one year, we demoted her to a lower-ranked position, and yet we left her pay level the same but frozen, pending a satisfactory performance review after another six months. You guessed it. She did not measure up and after two years she was terminated.

This story illustrates one of the worst kinds of employee problems any manager can face. A bad performer improperly trained, unjustifiably promoted and compensated, and unwilling to take the necessary steps for self-improvement is a tough nut to crack in today's world. In large part, this collection of prior errors in judgment made swift action impossible, but it was not her own fault—she had been misled and given undeserved encouragement and reward. For these reasons, immediate termination was not an option and even the measured steps we took were anything but satisfactory; they were certainly costly in many ways, not the least of which was the rotten apple-in-the-barrel phenomenon. I learned some time later that my predecessor had been involved in a romantic affair with the underachiever. Yet another giant management error!

A Day in the Life of Gerry and John . . .

"I believe I'm going to have to fire him, Gerry. I've tried everything, but the man just hasn't come up to par."

Jaime Alvarez was in Gerry Avilla's office, reporting on the status of the service department's monthly activities. Jaime was the service manager, with three foremen reporting to him, one in each of their locations. Things were going reasonably well, but one of the mechanics was not getting repairs done in the time allotted and quoted to the customer.

"He's gone through all the training, and is factory certified, right?"

"Yes, he passed all the tests, but lately he has been going downhill. Can't seem to get him to even realize why this is a problem."

"Just how bad are his times?"

"At least 10, maybe 15 percent over the prescribed time on most jobs. But he's 25 percent slower than our best men. Any ideas?"

"You know how expensive it is every time we have to hire and train a new man, Jaime? Find a way to get him up to par. Is his pay level appropriate? Maybe that's his problem."

"He's on the same level as the others with his experience. Won't qualify for the next level for another two years. I could tease him with the possibility of a raise, if you want."

"No promises though. They all get cost of living raises, so...Listen, give him the threat of termination if he doesn't shape up in...what? Another two months?"

"Will do."

As Jaime was leaving his boss's office, Gerry said, "Any chance he has personal problems, Jaime? You know how that can make difficulties for a guy."

"Everybody's got personal problems, Gerry. You, me, everybody. Geez, what are we supposed to be? Nursemaids?"

Gerry laughed. "Just do what you can. Talk to me about it again in a couple of weeks. Have him come see me if you think there's anything I can contribute, okay? Oh, and don't even think about looking around for a new guy until we're sure we need to make a move."

Jaime returned briefly and said, "I have already asked around, Gerry. I always have irons in the fire—you never know when somebody good might surface."

Gerry shrugged, and said, "I guess that's right. See you, Jaime."

Chapter 7

Orchestrate

There are lessons for managers in surprising places, including in the arts. Take note of the impressive performances of a high-quality symphony orchestra. Seventy or more men and women—each exquisitely trained as an individual instrumentalist—come together and rehearse for a unified delivery of a complex composition with one objective in mind: a public performance that comes close to perfection.

Sometime, make it a personal goal to attend the rehearsal sessions of a good orchestra. You will be amazed, I promise you, but you will also learn something profound; the precision with which the musicians finally deliver the magnificent end result does not come without a great deal of hard work by the conductor and by each and every instrumentalist as they practice their roles over and over.

Yes, to be sure, the sheet music gives very specific instructions to each player. These instructions are cryptic (they have to be), but they are unequivocal. The conductor may well introduce her own interpretation of the score, but the notes and symbols written by the composer and arranger are sacrosanct.

After a great deal of rehearsing, correcting errors for timing, and adjusting relative weight in each section (cluster of instruments), the orchestra is ready to deliver and the results are impressive. The surprising thing is often that during the actual performance the players seldom even look at the conductor. The reason is that they have been so well-orchestrated that they don't need to. It is on this part of the analogy you need to focus.

A manager's job is not to tell employees what to do, and especially not to tell how to do it—except in very lowly circumstances. What must be conveyed, and carefully orchestrated, are the desired results: consistent, predictable, and to a certain level of excellence. The leader's job then is to pick individuals with the talents and strengths that blend well together for a well-orchestrated outcome.

I can hear your protests; it is one thing to deliver a one-time performance that is well-orchestrated, but my team has to do it continuously, day in and day out. So how can that be a reasonable analogy to the orchestra?

You are right—it can't. And in addition, the business entity competes with other organizations in a tough and constantly changing environment. They also do not have the luxury of rehearsing. Every day for the business unit is performance day, and each employee must be on stage for an eight-hour or longer shift, contributing enthusiastically. Furthermore, the leader is not there (or should not be), in full view, providing constant guidance for each player when there's uncertainty. And, to add power to your argument, there is no score—or even a specific set of instructions in many cases—telling everyone exactly what to do. So the differences are real and compelling, but there's an important commonality; they (and you) want a well-coordinated outcome.

So build a solid understanding throughout your organization, top to bottom, about what you are trying to achieve (your mission), and push for a level of commitment to those objectives. You must find ways to ensure satisfaction of customers, cooperation and support from suppliers, and full involvement and commitment by employees at all levels. This is what I call orchestration!

The one best way for you to develop an orchestrated team is the same as it is in building a strong personal relationship. You must ensure complete **commitment**, which comes from **mutual trust**. **Trust** grows when you are **open, willing** to **listen** and **learn**, and you are **flexible**. These steps will enrich the workplace environment, making it one conducive to **winning**.

And anyway, you are the composer—so you can change the "score" to suit the circumstances. But do not change the score—or the rules of the game—without good reason, and never without inviting input.

And be sure to go through a constant process of review and evaluation, providing a flow of encouraging words to all the "performers" for their contribution. The orchestra gets reviewed by its audiences, and by the media critics. You get reviewed by those you serve! They may not applaud, but if you keep a close watch you will get their message in the form of repeat business, profits, growth, and expansion.

A Day in the Life of Gerry and John...

The shouting could be heard throughout the entire building: "Does anyone here know what they are doing? I drove all this way because I was told the part was in! Unbelievable! Let me talk to the parts manager, right now!"

Gerry Avilla emerged from his office, alarmed by the disturbance. He rushed into the parts department just in time to hear his parts manager, Doug Bellingham, greet the irate customer. "What seems to be the problem?" Doug asked calmly. He was not the type to get upset.

Gerry waited a moment to see if he could learn what—if anything—had gone wrong.

"I'll tell you what the problem is. A part we need to keep a tractor operating went astray in shipment. So it was reordered by you guys three days ago, and we were told that the part came in late yesterday afternoon, so here I am to pick it up. But one of your incompetent people sold it to someone else. That's what the problem is."

Doug turned to the embarrassed-looking counter man and said, "Did you sell the part, Jim? Was it in the hold bin?"

"Yes, Doug. I mean, no, it wasn't in the hold bin. I found it on the appropriate inventory shelf and sold it first thing this morning." He turned to the customer and said, "I'm real sorry, sir. This is an item we sell very few of, so the normal stock level is just one unit, and—"

"I don't care what your normal stocking level is, I was told the part was here for me, and I expect you people to tell me the truth. So now what are you going to do? We have a tractor sitting idle for a week and…"

Gerry had stepped forward, now understanding the predicament: "I'll tell you what we'll do, sir. We'll deliver a loaner tractor to your site immediately. And then, when the part comes in, I'll have the driver deliver it to your site, where he'll install the part and bring back the loaner. No charge, of course, and I am very sorry. We try hard to avoid these kinds of errors, but we'll make it right immediately."

The customer left, consoled and yet not feeling totally happy with what had happened. A tractor down in a busy seeding season was costly. He was grateful for the solution, but still…

Gerry asked Doug Bellingham to step into his office and closed the door. "How does this happen, Doug?" he said calmly. "It happened once before, a couple of months ago, and I thought you had a handle on the correct procedure."

"Gerry, I am truly sorry. I'll get to the bottom of this situation, and see who screwed up, but when parts come in from the DAE factory they are coded as 'presold' or 'for stock,' as you know. We unpack and store them according to that code. But this one was trans-shipped from another dealer's inventory. It was not coded."

"And someone didn't bother to check the 'pre-sold' list. That it?"

"Looks that way, boss. I'll get everybody focused on the issue. It won't happen again."

"Make sure it doesn't. The fix for this is expensive, Doug. In more ways than one."

"I know. And thanks for solving the problem."

"The problem's not solved until you prevent it from happening again. So get to it!"

Chapter 8

Cheerleading

This is also a short subject, and one that may seem anomalous to some readers. It may seem trivial to others, but I see cheerleading as a vital role of all good managers. In fact, I am so convinced of the importance of this that I actually see the cheerleading role as a central one in every leadership role, even that of the United States presidency. Let me go a step further, and add that for the sitting president nothing is more important than being a good cheerleader—*nothing*.

I am not talking about razzle-dazzle here, or in any way suggesting theatrical performances by you (or the U.S. president) to get folks pumped and primed. I am talking about being positive and enthusiastic at all times—giving your people every reason to feel confident and ready to take on challenges. Not in a phony way, but by trying to avoid negative behaviors, scowls, cursing, tantrums, or showing disgust or disappointment in a team player. As I have said before, do your criticizing by being specific in the ways an error affects your outcomes, and do so in private.

There is absolutely nothing wrong with showing open disappointment or other emotions to your team when something goes wrong. In fact, it lets everyone know that you are human and real. But always, always put it in terms that are specific and meaningful. If you say such things as "That is just the pits, guys! It will be tough to overcome that setback any time soon," (for a lost contract, say, or something equally significant) then it is too vague. But even this kind of open display can be useful if it is put in positive terms, and if it is sincere (remember that trust is vital, and can only come from sincerity). Why not follow such an open statement as the one I mentioned: "But I have faith that you guys will do your best to see to it that we get the so-and-so account…right? Are we on track with that?" Or something appropriate that encourages.

This is the key—and it is a huge part of your responsibility to always look on the bright side even when things look bleak. To not do so is a certain step in the direction of failure or at least failure to build a winning culture.

Illustration

No matter your political leanings, you have to admit that the general approach of President Ronald Reagan was always in sharp contrast to that of President Jimmy Carter. Carter referred to "A culture of malaise…" having engulfed the country, at a time when things looked bleak and everyone needed to hear something more encouraging. By contrast, Reagan always found something uplifting to say, even when confronted by massive worldwide challenges. Be that way in your setting and see what a difference it can make. It is a vital step in building your winning culture. But be sure that your actions, and your display of emotions, do not undermine your own message.

A Day in the Life of Gerry and John . . .

Gerry asked John to bring everyone up to the lobby for a brief meeting. "Make it 10 minutes to five tonight. I have an important announcement to make."

"You going to tell me what the subject is, Gerry?"

"Sure. I'm going to announce the big deal you landed. And thank everyone for the part they played in getting the deal, and asking them for their continued focus. Ten minutes max. Okay?"

"Great! Good idea Gerry. A little positive talk is always good."

The brief meeting went well, and everyone seemed cheered by the news, since the economic downturn had caused concerns. But as John drove home that night, he found himself wondering what had induced Gerry to think of the pep talk. Most unusual, and out of character for Gerry, he thought. *I'll have to ask him,* he thought. *Sometime when the time is right.*

Chapter 9

Lower the Cultural Boundaries

As discussed in the introduction, there are quite natural boundaries between subcultures inside any organization. The departmental issues and challenges—and the various backgrounds of people in each department—assure that such differences will always exist. It is important therefore to remember and counteract the propensity of American businesses to promote people vertically. Many Eastern businesses cross-train more fully than we do, and this further ensures that people will (or can) readily see the challenges faced by those in a different department. It's the old adage of "walk a mile in someone else's shoes," so take heed of this reality and confront it, openly, often, and with the objective in mind of lowering the intercultural boundaries. There are a few specific recommendations below, but you will no doubt dream up others that best suit your particular circumstances.

❖ Be inclusive (invite accountants to sit in on marketing meetings, for example).

❖ Encourage interaction: formal and informal.

❖ Show empathy often.

❖ Share information widely, such as celebrations and rewards.

❖ Reinforce behaviors that help bring down barriers.

❖ Show appreciation often. Go out of your way to do so.

❖ Encourage input, especially on how employees handle their assignment.

❖ Make any criticism only in private, and always show how a failure affects something in specific terms. Avoid vague generalities like "You're letting the team down."

❖ Spend some time with all employees: guiding, encouraging, but also showing great and genuine interest in them as people, fathers, mothers, community members, whole people.

On the latter item, Peters and Waterman (*In Search of Excellence*, 1982) recommend "management by walking around." They suggest that good leaders spend time away from their own desk, on the battlefield with the "troops," because their presence is valuable; not as someone checking up on things but as a colleague genuinely interested in the people on the team and how things are going.

A final point on the topic of culture. This is a huge subject; one on which many whole books have been written. In chapter 19 of this book, you'll find additional information and tips. Culture is an all-encompassing concept with sweeping and powerful impact on how a group functions and how it interacts with other groups. The collective milieu can be uniformly positive or negative, or mixed, with negative elements lurking here and there like a single out-of-tune violin in an orchestra. You must be acutely aware of the many cultural realities within your group, team, or department, and work hard on eliminating the negative influences. Such variables will inevitably undermine your chances of developing a winning culture. So come to terms with which cultural clashes exist and cultivate a shared commitment to improvement by encouraging interdepartmental (as well as interpersonal) cooperation.

A Day in the Life of Gerry and John . . .

John Standish was still working on the agenda for the sales meeting planned for tomorrow afternoon. It was late in the day, and he was tired and felt like heading home. Just as he was closing down his computer Doug Bellingham stuck his head in the door and asked, "Got a few minutes, John?"

"Yeah, sure. What's up, Doug?"

Doug sat down and said, "I heard you're having a sales meeting, and wanted to suggest something. Don't take offense, but I'd like some of my guys to sit in on one of your meetings sometime. Me too...but not necessarily tomorrow if your agenda is full."

John hesitated. "What made you think of doing that, my friend? Anybody in your department have ideas of becoming sales reps?"

Doug laughed nervously. "Not that I know of," he said, "but I suppose that's always a possibility. No, it just occurred to me that we are all in the same boat, in a way. We are here to service the needs of customers. Sometimes we...I mean those of us in parts—and service too, I'd guess—don't quite see the obvious commonalities among us all. What brought it on was I overheard two of my guys saying negative things about the salespeople. They may not get what the challenges are, instead seeing your folks as just getting fat commissions and expense accounts. Know what I mean, John?"

John leaned back in his chair and thought for a moment. "You know, Doug, you might be onto something. We really are all on the same team, and I'd guess my guys don't often come around and see what your problems are either, do they? Not even me…and I should. I know that."

"Well, I'm glad you're receptive to the idea. You are always welcome to come to our get-togethers. We usually have semiformal meetings on things once a month. How about your meeting tomorrow? Any problem if-"

"Nah. No problem at all. As a matter of fact I welcome a few of your guys. Two or three each time. I'll try to make them welcome, and encourage their participation. We are going to end the meeting at six, tell them. We'll send out for some pizza and bring in some beer after we're done with the formalities. You got enough room in your budget for an hour of overtime for three of your people? We can take another two or three next time."

"Yes, my budget's in good shape. I should clear it with Gerry though. He might not see the purpose."

"Great. I'll talk to Gerry also. Thanks for the suggestion, Doug. Good thinking."

Two days later, Doug came back to talk with John, and he said that the three men he'd asked to attend the sales meeting thoroughly enjoyed it. Two said it gave them new insights into the challenges faced by salespeople, and the other started asking what he would have to do to become eligible for a job in sales.

John laughed. "Have him come and talk to me, Doug. Hey, and next time, how about you come to the meeting yourself. You don't get overtime though!"

Chapter 10

Matchups

This is a favorite topic of mine, and it is hugely important. Consider this: If you were a tennis player of average amateur ability (as I am), and you were asked to play as a doubles partner with one of the world's best professional players, what chance is there that: a) you would beat any good team? b) you would find the experience enjoyable or beneficial? c) the hotshot would invite you to play another match with him ever?

The answer is obvious, right? There is such a mismatch in this improbable scenario that no possible good could come of such a combination. By contrast, incidentally, for the past several years the men's number one tennis team in the world has been the Bryan Brothers (Mike and Bob Bryan are identical twins). Most tennis experts are certain that their success has come from their ability to communicate well, each knowing the other's strengths and weaknesses, each covering for the other resolutely.

In all businesses and other organizations where workers interact and combine their efforts, the matchups you create must be handled very carefully. Personality clashes can be disastrous—producing rancor and discord—but also, so can different levels of training and education or markedly different levels of maturity.

Maturity—as used in this context—does not refer to chronological age, but is a measure of openness and willingness to be interdependent (see chapter 19). Immature people tend to be self-oriented and unwilling to share credit, blame, or accountability. A winning culture can be thwarted by such negative subtleties, so do your best to bring team players together with the right mix of ingredients to produce compatibility and mutual respect. This is hard to accomplish, I know, but critical.

There are situations where a mix of experiences can be of value, of course, and may be especially conducive to the training and development of younger team members. But these kinds of mixes should be openly recognized and defined, and the mentoring process eagerly embraced (see chapter 2 on mentoring).

For purposes here I want to deal with yet another aspect of matchups. I refer to the obvious but often overlooked need to match each employee with assignments that fit their abilities and experiences.

As I said, this seems axiomatic—perhaps even automatic—and yet there are many people floundering in jobs that are too big for them so they become discouraged, and others with far more ability than they can use in their current assignment—so they become bored and unenthusiastic. The latter is, in fact, the worst of these two situations, but be on your guard against creating or ignoring either of these mismatches.

The whole concept of job growth, and the importance of encouragement, is one that could fill a book much larger than this one without even touching on the theory. So I will try to be brief. First, however, is a true-to-life example of my major point about discouragement and its consequences.

Illustration

I have a son who played ice hockey as a boy. He was good, and he made the traveling teams since age eight. He even played up in a higher age group sometimes. In my eager desire to help him continue to grow in the sport, I carefully pointed out his errors after each game (at the time I thought I was being helpful). His development seemed to stagnate, however, and then coincidentally I began studying motivation theory, and slowly the light went on. I stopped identifying errors and offered only praise and encouragement for the things he did well. His game improved noticeably and he seemed to regain his old enthusiasm for the sport. In fact, he is still playing ice hockey today, several decades later.

Your role is in part that of a motivator and—where appropriate—also that of a teacher. If you have direct experience and expertise in an area that pertains to the assignments of people you supervise, avoid the temptation to tell them how to do their job. Try to focus on desirable outcomes and in an appropriate way match the challenges you present to them with their current level of development. By all means, challenge them, but if they do not reach your ideal levels right away, be patient. Compliment any and all growth that does take place and be sure to stretch each person just a little, not too much; they will be motivated to grow in their job as the job itself grows. And they will reach higher.

Having said that it is important for people to receive encouragement, I must acknowledge that some kinds of work provide built-in rewards. Anything with tangible outcomes would be an example, such as sales, or any work that creates a product or fixes problems. But even then, there's always merit in a supervisor's pat on the back for a job well done.

Self-contained job enrichment (yes that's what it really is if you have an assignment with built-in rewards) is not always possible. It may not be, for instance, for someone who works on an assembly line, attaching part A to part B hundreds of times per day, with no real awareness of what the end product is or does. So in such a set of circumstances, managers certainly should reward consistently good performance with praise and with expressions of gratitude.

In such a potentially dull routine as the one I mention above, however, you can have opportunities for enrichment that help you sustain high levels of commitment. One possibility is in encouraging such workers to become trainers of others, or to lead discussions on improvements in the workplace, in formal and informal settings. You can also give them a change of assignment if they are amenable, but do not push people who do not wish to be stretched, and don't punish them for their choice. At some future date they may change their desires. Be ready to help them grow when that time comes.

A less common problem occurs when people are in jobs that are too small for them. Such a situation can occur, and nothing is more discouraging or so destructive of morale. You might ask what kind of person would allow themselves to be in such a predicament, and all I can say is that I have seen it—though not often. Lack of confidence could explain it, which can be a personality issue, but it can also come from the failure of a boss to encourage people, or from giving too little praise when it is earned. Even the most self-confident person welcomes praise.

As a final word on this subject, be alert to potential mismatches of every kind on your team. Stimulate people who can rise to the challenge, and encourage them to stretch. Be sure you create enough variety to make even the most repetitive work occasionally different. Do not impose heavy burdens on those who cannot carry them reasonably, but also do not hesitate in allowing those with an aggressive leaning to take on more responsibility when appropriate. These are among the most critical responsibilities for all managers, and if wrongly handled, they can prevent the development of a winning culture.

A Day in the Life of Gerry and John . . .

Gerry had interviewed several people for the office manager's job, including a woman named Barbara King, and John had also spent a little time with her. They were both impressed with her credentials; she had a bachelor's degree in business and accounting from a good university, and had passed half the examinations that would lead to a CPA certification. Furthermore, she had worked in a similar position in a large automobile dealership. But she seemed somewhat timid to both of them—strangely so.

They were discussing Barbara's suitability, comparing her with the other candidates they had seen so far, and couldn't seem to reach an agreement between them.

"I like the guy who had actually worked in our industry, Gerry," John said. "At least he would be up to speed on the job quicker, and would be more likely to hang around for a few years. He'd also demand a lower salary. That's worth something. Do we really need a CPA?"

"Barbara actually told me she was not necessarily going to complete the CPA, John. So that question seems moot. She likes our location, as she lives close by. She's a single mother, so my guess is she'd hang around a long time. The other guy is a better match, though, I'll give you that. But there was just something quirky...I didn't feel comfortable with him."

"But what do you make of Barbara's passive personality, Gerry? She seems very nice, almost too nice, and this is not a quiet place at times. There are some strong characters working here. Some of them might offend her, I'm thinking."

"I spoke with the GM at the Ford dealership. Barbara worked there for four years and did a good job. He said she warms up and becomes more assertive after she adapts to the situation. Before that job she was an accountant in another car dealership for a year or two."

"Why did she leave?"

"Commute time problems. She now has a child in school...I'm quite satisfied with her explanation of her needs in that area. She can be home in five minutes from here, in an emergency situation and also on an everyday basis."

"Well, you're the boss, Gerry. You decide. I'd go the other way, but will not fight you on it if you want to hire her. Might be good to have a woman in that job for a change. She's too qualified, that's for sure, as there are only a dozen people she's responsible for, even if you include Jake (the credit and collections man), but if she's willing to accept our pay level, and knows there's no future promotion potential...Did you ask her about that?"

"Not directly, no. But she has seen our organization chart, such as it is, and has looked at the financial figures over the last five years. She must know there's no promotion possible. From what I understand, she could conceivably complete the CPA in another year or so...so I have to admit that she could be just using us as a stopgap until she gets that done."

"And then we'd be left holding the bag again in another year or two. Searching for someone to replace her, I mean."

Gerry picked up all the applicant résumés and leafed through them. "Other than Barbara and the guy you like, there's slim picking here," he said. "Let me sleep on it—I'll make a decision tomorrow."

Chapter 11

Trust Building

In an earlier section I discussed the tendency of many managers to spend more of their time with selected individuals: usually the winners on their team, the high achievers, or those with whom they share common interests. While this is natural, it is generally unwise and can be quite damaging in subtle ways. A perception of favoritism is created, and often that perception is valid. There is nothing more valuable in building and sustaining any relationship than trust. And do not mistake trust for predictability, though there are some commonalities.

Everyone wants their automobile to be trustworthy, to start and run without difficulty day in and day out. Predictability is hugely important in this form of trust. Similarly, in a personal relationship and under a given set of circumstances, predictability is critical—but there's a catch. An entirely predictable relationship can be boring for many people. Change and excitement—or at least freshness—can make such a difference to any relationship, working or personal, so spice up your predictability with a little imagination to produce some level of freshness and joy. Be creative.

But the one thing that must not be undermined or weakened is loyalty. Two-way loyalty in all relationships, personal or otherwise, is vital for mutual enrichment and satisfaction. Loyalty develops slowly and is based on mutual trust…but it can be fragile, and can evaporate rapidly. So how is such mutual trust built and sustained? The four most common errors made in the workplace that undermine trust in an organizational setting are:

Inconsistency. People need to be treated in consistent ways on all the things that matter most. Any one of us can have a bad day, and based on mood alone we can be unpredictable, but if we allow (yes, it is a choice we make) this to significantly alter the way we treat others in ordinary exchanges then trust is potentially undermined.

Insincerity. If a manager frequently praises an employee—with no criticism on any aspect of their work—and then in a formal performance review makes only critical observations, such a reversal will result in the loss of trust. So be sure you deliver no surprises in a negative direction, as they reflect insincerity. Surprises in a positive direction are always welcomed and often of value.

Secrecy. In every organization there's need to be appropriately careful about certain kinds of information, but erring on the side of openness is always better than the opposite. When people feel left out they invent their own information and will often spread potentially damaging misinformation in the form of rumors. This is one of the most insidious manifestations of a lack of trust.

Favoritism. We all have favorites. To deny this is to deny human nature, but in the workplace all evident forms of favoritism seriously undermine the winning culture. There's no room for it—no exceptions. People who achieve must be recognized, of course, but when you do this be certain of the justice and the justifiability of such recognition and reward. Spell out your rationale openly, or the worst will be assumed. Think carefully about how you treat all of your people. Equally importantly, communicate your concerns on this topic openly with all the other supervisory personnel about this form of openness, and welcome feedback from others.

The other problem with spending more time with the winners on your team is that it takes time away from those who need your attention the most. Highly productive people need less supervision, generally, and even a little less encouragement than those not doing quite so well, so you should see to it that your time is apportioned on the basis of need. I know it is a hackneyed saying, but it is nevertheless true: A team is only as strong as its weakest player, so build your team's overall effectiveness by strengthening those less able, less confident, and less experienced.

Some might see these recommendations as being too soft, and that behaving in the ways I suggest will invite employees to take advantage of you. There is always a risk of being "used" in any open system. I acknowledge this reality, but despite such risks the benefits far outweigh the negatives. Furthermore, some people are more fragile than others, and some respond to uncertainty and challenge better than others. So do any fine-tuning that seems indicated in your setting, by all means, but you can be certain of one thing: If you are guilty of any of the above listed trust-busting behaviors, your hopes for a winning culture will evaporate.

A Day in the Life of Gerry and John . . .

Gerry asked John to join him at his golf club for lunch one day, and he raised a subject that had come up before, several years back, but in vague terms. Now it sounded much more concrete:

"How would you feel about us giving our attorney a small percentage of ownership in the business, John? She does such a great job on our taxes and such, and, well, I'm not talking a big percentage."

"She already gets a fat fee for everything she does, Gerry—as all lawyers do."

John barely knew the attorney Gerry was talking about, and yet he knew that Gerry spent a lot of his spare time with the woman, and played golf with her at least twice a month.

"Well, here's the thing. If she gets a percentage, say just 5 percent, she said she would reduce her fees on everything she does for us."

"Wait a minute. You've already discussed this with her? Without my involvement?"

Gerry looked alarmed. "Well just in tentative terms, John. And I told her I'd have to get your agreement on it anyway. We have talked about having others become minority shareholders, you know that."

"Ages ago, Gerry. We talked about it so long ago I thought it was a dead issue. Now...you've sure surprised me, Gerry. I thought we communicated well enough that surprises like this would never be a problem between us."

"Look, I'm sorry. I should have asked for your input first. But it came up spontaneously, and...I really am sorry. Let's not spoil lunch. We can think about it some, on our own, and then talk again in a few days. Okay, pal? Waiter, bring me the check please."

Chapter 12

Feature the Benefits

As a young engineer I made an early transition to marketing, and was given responsibility for training sales and management personnel on the technical aspects of our products (industrial and mining machinery). This was business-to-business, of course, where the buying decisions tend to be substantially more pragmatic than in the consumer arena, so the keys to success were in showing customers exactly how they would gain from buying our products. I came up with what I thought was a succinct and clever training edict for that setting, one that still has merit: **To benefit from features, feature the benefits**.

No one buys anything unless they think there is some gain to be made—that is axiomatic. What separates business-to-business (B-to-B) marketing challenges (largely, but not exclusively) from those in the consumer-direct marketplace is that consumers' gains are often intangible or even imagined. The savvy buyer in an industrial setting especially wants to know exactly what your products and services will do to improve their efficiencies, reduce their headaches, or maximize opportunity for them. The features of your product have to translate directly into such gains or there's no incentive to buy from you, even with all the charms your salespeople may possess.

Furthermore, even consumers do not buy many items just to own them; they have to see benefits. There are exceptions to this, of course, such as in the oddly fascinating world of collectors (antiques, artworks, specialty, and curiosities), but even there a partial motivation is often the potential gains from appreciation in value. No one buys an electric drill, though, simply to own the drill. They want what the drill will do for them. They may want the prestige (real or imagined) of owning a certain make of designer clothing, shoes by a famous maker, or an automobile considered luxury class, to name just a few goods made mostly successful without having specific or needed tangible benefits. But you get the message, and if you keep a sharp eye on your TV, you will witness many dollars spent on advertisements that have appeal, and may be creative and funny. But do they always feature the benefits, even indirectly?

Illustration

One currently running TV advertising series serves as a good example of what I recommend, even while being simple and humorous. The scene is a golf course. Real-world golf pro Davis Love and his caddy are contemplating a lengthy putt, with Davis keenly focused as he reads the green. The caddy suddenly says, "Don't even think about three-putting, Davis. Not with all that money on the line." Then comes the advertiser's message: "Make sure the people on your team are on your side and understand your needs..." It's an advertisement by a consulting firm of some sort. A great message well-delivered!

So what and how can we learn from these revelations?

This question is easily answered, but it is often difficult to apply such answers. And yet this is the key to success in the whole process of bringing goods and services to market, in promoting them effectively, and even in dropping items from your line when the time is right. So here are some general guidelines for readers to think about and apply to their own setting.

Don't allow your people to get hung up on the features of your products unless those features can be shown to serve some purpose of direct benefit to your potential customers.

Do try hard to be honest about how your features stack up against those of your competitors, and find ways to modify or improve the feature set of your own goods. Or, offset any competitor's advantages with other features you can legitimately claim of greater value to the buyer.

Don't forget that in most arenas today, things change rapidly. This is especially true in consumer electronics, for example, and all other hi-tech areas, but very few products remain viable and equally valuable throughout their cycle of acceptability and desirability.

Do come to terms with exactly where your products are in the inevitable cycle of marketplace desirability. Very few products can sustain high levels of sales forever, and you must be ready to transition to replacements when marketplace conditions are ripe. You can be proactive in this, or reactive, depending on your agility and reaction costs.

Don't forget that some low profitability items can have synergistic benefits for you (by partly absorbing overheads, for example, or in fulfilling a full range of customer needs synergistically), and must therefore remain in the mix of items you offer when past their peak of demand.

Do remember that your marketing messages should all consistently feature benefits—especially in B-to-B arenas. But be sure there is always an equally important key to your continued success: integrity. The claims you make about benefits must prove reliable, and you must back them up in tangible (benefit-laden) ways. A winning culture is one in which all personnel have high levels of integrity in this—and it begins with you!

Occasionally you can depart from the edict of focusing on benefits rather than features just a little—if you conform to my edict most of the time—with teasers or fanciful ideas and "gingerbread" claims or promotions. One example that comes to mind is the classy and warmly received Christmastime TV commercial that Budweiser uses effectively. A horse does remarkable things such as retrieving the branch of a tree like how a dog fetches a stick. It is purely fun and charmingly attractive. Such a sparingly used promo adds warmth and humanity to the invisible corporate face. But this too is a benefit of a different sort, isn't it?

Finally, and most importantly, **don't** forget the significance of internal marketing. For your team to be effective, all of your personnel have to be sold on what your business offers. Make no assumptions other than this: It all begins inside. A winning culture is one in which there is genuine commitment of every kind and at every level. Everyone is responsible for sales.

Illustration

There's yet another TV commercial that illustrates, I think, the broader issues associated with everyone being sold on and proud of the product. It is a General Electric jet aircraft engines scenario, showing workers assembling their complex products on the shop floor. Then the scene switches to an unidentified airfield, with the big four-engine Boeing passenger plane taking off. The camera pans around to the lineup of GE factory workers watching with pride, many with tears in their eyes. They are sold on what they do for a living.

By the way, I'm not sure the general public is tuned in to the significance of this kind of message, so paying the price for advertising a product that has a narrow vertical market in a huge horizontal marketplace makes much sense. Put it down to "image" marketing perhaps. It is expensive, and the results are intangible, yet this is often done by large corporations.

A Day in the Life of Gerry and John . . .

John Standish was in his office one day, checking the sales call reports, and he couldn't help overhearing Ned Baxter, one of his salesmen, talking to a customer in a cubicle set aside for the salesmen to use when they were in the office. One of the salespeople would serve as the "on-deck" guy each day, but most of the time they were all out in their territories.

"You see in this illustration, Mr. Galanta, this tractor engine has a double overhead camshaft, making it virtually the only one in the industry, in an engine of this class and size, that is. The crankshaft is also flame-hardened, something else you'll not find on a competitive machine. You saw how comfortable the seat is in the operator's compartment, and you also made mention of the comprehensive instrument cluster. Are there any other questions, or can I get you to say yes on this? We have just that one in inventory, and the next available off the line will come in three weeks down the road. They sell well, you know, so it will be gone soon. But this one is ready to go the minute you give me the go-ahead. We could have it in your hands tomorrow first thing. Delivery is included in the price I gave you."

John then heard the customer say, "Well, I'll just have to go home and do some figuring, Ned. I'll call you if I decide to go ahead." He wondered if Ned needed some extra help on this sale, but then John's phone rang. By the time he got off the line, the customer had left already.

Chapter 13

Budgeting Downfalls

Every organization needs a budget to help guide their activities. A meaningful budget begins with an attempt to estimate potential revenues. This measure comes from the sales forecast, of course, and then it can progress to answering the question "What resources do we need to attain these revenue targets?" These are the basic underlying drivers of the budget process, and I don't need to get into the nuts and bolts of this here. Instead, let me point out some vagaries of the budgeting process itself that many organizations face, and the most common mistakes made by managers in getting through the budgeting process. Some of these are the most damaging influences on a winning culture.

Whose job is it to create the budget?

The best answer is "Everyone's!" Yes, I do mean **everyone**. Budgets that are imposed on workers from the ivory towers, by "bean counters" or other administrative levels, are always destructive, and they always undermine commitment!

But surely you don't want every individual deciding how much to spend in every small account; how much money to allocate to this or that activity?

No, not exactly. But a collaborative bottom-up effort is called for and produces the best chance that people at every level will feel like an active participant in the organization's activities and objectives. Furthermore, they are then more likely to take ownership in it and be careful in their adherence or departure. This is vital for a winning culture to develop.

In each department, planning should be seen as a shared responsibility. In the days when Management By Objectives (MBO) was a guiding philosophy for managers, researchers discovered that the key to success was not "What Objectives?" but "Whose?" Many studies showed that imposed goals are better than none at all, but goals set collaboratively (with shared ownership) are the most likely to produce high levels of commitment. And, surprisingly perhaps, people tend to impose higher targets on themselves than would otherwise be imposed by their superiors—but only in circumstances where employees feel there is an open, trusting environment.

One of the greatest weaknesses in the budgeting processes for business, and certainly for governments, is the tendency to use prior history and simply add a growth factor to all accounts. If we spent X dollars on advertising last year, then this year we should spend X plus a growth factor. This approach trivializes the budget, and the whole notion of planning is demeaned.

Zero-based budgeting has been tried again and again, and although the merits of it are widely recognized, it often fails miserably. Why?

Zero-based budgeting can only work in situations where there is absolute trust and freedom from turf-protecting behaviors—in other words, in very mature settings. This calls for everyone to be willing to diminish their own importance when such is desirable or indicated. Yes, cut your own budget if it is justified! How many would do such a thing? Would you?

An organization is a complex *organism*. As with any organic entity, there are imbalances of every kind, newly emerging ones and old ones that just never seem to get corrected. Perfection is not possible, but there is no reason to abandon it as an ideal target. As a leader, you must strive to be aware of all the existing imbalances so that you can openly adjust and compensate, all the while letting everyone have their say, and all the while keeping everyone informed about the decisions you made and why you made them.

Illustration

During the middle of my career, I was a profit center manager for a large corporation, one of more than 40 around the globe. Each of these scattered businesses did many millions of dollars annual business, and each was responsible for their own budgeting. They were genuine profit centers with autonomy over expenditures of every kind—until things got tight, such as in a cyclical downturn in the economy. The typical way of dealing with a recession for that corporation and many others was to impose from the top across-the-board cuts in several expense accounts and to freeze hiring. Sounds good, right?

But hold on. Because these decentralized business units varied in their cost containment, and especially in head count, a freeze or a cut for those already operating on a lean budget was punitive and even destructive. For those operating more loosely, a cut of any kind was easier to handle.

Such are the vagaries of mishandled, top-down budgeting edicts.

So be smart about budgeting. Try to encourage input from the lowest possible level. This is valid advice for all decision making, but especially budget-process decisions, because people at every level are directly affected by such decisions in very personal ways; all must live within the dictates attached.

Speaking of cost containment, and other aspects of efficiency, I used to tell my students—who were eager for advice on how to build a successful career—that I had more than once literally eliminated my own job. It's true! I found ways to improve efficiencies or create synergies in ways that made my own position redundant. Not once did this result in my termination, however. Who would fire such a selfless person, one who could or would continue to seek organizational improvements? No one would, and yet this kind of thing happens too seldom. Instead, people tend to protect their own turf, even attempt to enhance their own power. The typical budgeting process invites such selfish behaviors, rewards guilty parties, and undermines attempts to build a winning culture.

The budgeting process is fraught with dangers of the kind I mention, and yet it is the one area where it is relatively easy—with careful thought and analysis—to ensure shared and equitable participation.

- ❖ Do not *impose* budgets.

- ❖ Do not use the budgeting process for rewards or punishment.

- ❖ Do not forget what the budget is: a road map. And everyone on board is travelling the same road, or they should be if a winning culture is to be built and sustained.

The following chapter is closely related to the foregoing, as it has to do with how well the organization is doing in measurable terms: How well the road map is being followed.

A Day in the Life of Gerry and John . . .

Several months had passed, and the new office manager was doing a good job already. In fact, she had prepared a summary current year deviance report and a preliminary budget for the following year, and had even checked with the UCLA business school economic forecasting unit to see what the potentials were for the agricultural equipment segment of the economy in the area. Gerry had made a few adjustments after a brief conversation with John Standish, and was now presenting the budget to all the department heads in a closed meeting.

"Okay, listen up. Last item on the agenda for today is the budget. I have just given you the new budget for next year. Last year we went over on a number of expense items and it cost us profits. Some of your bonuses were affected by that, so I know you'll want to make sure we are on target next year." Gerry paused at that point and slowly looked around the table, a grim expression on his face. "There's every reason to believe these revenue targets are attainable, but I want you to know that if revenues in any one area go higher than these figures I will listen to an appeal for more expenditures to match. Barbara has developed a new reporting system that will be more up-to-date and more reliable, making your job of staying on track that much easier. So take these figures as preliminary, but unless there's a serious objection from anyone I'd like to firm up this budget as soon as possible. The bank has asked for this, so that we can extend our credit lines a bit, so get back to me with any serious concerns by Friday, okay? Otherwise, this is our plan for the year."

Chapter 14

Efficiency and Your Vital Signs

When you go to the doctor, your vital signs are checked: heart rate, blood pressure, body mass index, or blood sugar level. Basically, all the vital signs of human health. Businesses also have "vital signs" that can tell managers a great deal about the health of their organization and indicate the need for corrective action. Most are simply labeled "ratios," or more correctly, "conversion ratios."

There is no particular magic in any one ratio, although some are more powerful measures than others of course. Most business leaders become acutely aware of their profitability ratios, such as returns-on-assets (ROA) or returns-on-invested capital (ROI), and net income as a percentage of revenues and so on, without realizing that sometimes these indicators can be inadequate or even misleading. Let me expand some more on this in discussing the vital signs of business.

Growth is a desirable goal for most businesses (and I have devoted chapter 18 to some special aspects of it), but growth itself has dangerous traps and vagaries attached. If your current resources are being underutilized, then growth will improve most of your resource conversion ratios, naturally enough, but if you have to grow your resources in order to produce more revenue (at some stage in the life of a successful business this is inevitable), you may inadvertently create insurmountable difficulties.

Let's take inventory as one resource example. Assume your business model is such that you have inventories turning over at an annual rate of 5:1, and you see an opportunity to grow. If you are to retain the same inventory-turn ratio you will need to invest in more inventory, using either external sources to fund the growth (using a line of credit, perhaps a loan or a fresh investment, or by diverting from your own retained earnings). The temptation may be to try to improve your inventory-turnover ratio to 6:1, and that might be possible. Improving any conversion ratio sounds like a great idea, but such a move could conceivably result in customer dissatisfaction if you are out of stock from time to time, so be cautious. Here are five critical things involving inventory management:

- ❖ Do frequent *item-by-item* analyses of how your inventory moves, and take action.

- ❖ Develop an appreciation for the potential *synergies* of even low-turning items.

- ❖ Don't push for improved inventory turns at the expense of customer satisfaction.

❖ Make inventory control efficiencies a regular topic of management discussions.

❖ Clear out (write off or scrap) items that do not sell. Dead wood destroys performance.

Inventories are not the only balance sheet item that absorbs assets, though in some businesses it is a big one. Receivables can be similarly greedy. Your business model needs to be fine-tuned in such a way that you collect money due to you as aggressively as possible without losing the goodwill of your customers. Do aging analyses frequently, and take decisive action with old and "dead" receivable accounts. Examine your terms carefully. If you give discounts for prompt payment, make certain you are "in tune" with competitors and industry-wide practices. Balance your relationship with customers against your own need for both on-time revenues and an efficient ratio of collections. If you need to change policies, do so openly and honestly. And finally, be willing to take a realistic approach to uncollectable accounts.

And then there's payables. I recently read that an audit of the City of Los Angeles revealed losses in interest burdens exceeding $1 million per year because they paid bills *before the due date*. Your accounts payable people can be overly efficient too. Make this an automatic efficiency measure to be tracked and reported regularly.

Every item on your balance sheet (both sides) must be monitored faithfully. Every time you sell something, and every time you buy something or pay for a service, your balance sheet changes. Yes, every time! You may not actually see your balance sheet more than once a year, but you should have it in mind at all times. All the items, on both the liability side and the assets side, are in constant fluctuation.

Take debts, for example. Your organization gains much by having debt, as it leverages your capital positively. But debt must be serviced at a cost that must be factored into your budget. You may be able to hold on to customers by having low-turn items in inventory, or by granting generous credit terms, but these should be seen as reservoirs of money sitting idle until liquidated. Conversely, don't push for better turnover of any asset at the expense of goodwill or worse: lost revenues. There's a correct balance for every account, so make sure you and all your people understand this balance. Yes, people at virtually every level can help make this process effective. Train them and reward them for recognizing and reporting indications that the vital signs are deteriorating.

Many business leaders pay more attention to their income statement than they do to their balance sheet, but both can and should regularly steer your decision making. Remember that every transaction in business instantly changes your balance sheet for better or worse. Every sale, every purchase, every check you write, every payment you receive, every item in "raw materials" that gets processed, and much more. They all affect the balance of assets and liabilities instantly. It is not just the responsibility of your controller or your accounting staff to watch these changes and evaluate them. Everyone in a managerial or supervisory role needs to be a participant. You can overdo this vigilance, obviously, but do not avoid it. It's an important part of every manager's job, and every employee can be made aware of the consequences of their choices and actions too. It adds to their appreciation for their role, and to their sense of belonging, their growth. Employees in winning organizations have "roles," not just jobs or tasks.

I have not dealt with the topic of expense controls here, simply because this often gets plenty of attention from managers at every level, for the obvious reasons. Instead, I have focused on the less visible aspect of resource conversion. These measures, and similar fine-tuning on numerous vital signs, are the nitty-gritty of building an effective and efficient organization. One that not only focuses on maximization, but does so in ways that fill real needs in the marketplace and produce good outcomes for all parties involved. The human component is (or should be) always uppermost in your mind, but the relationship between human thought and action and the various material measures of success is foundational. So train your people to be on the lookout for ways to improve all your vital signs. Reward them for being proactive!

A Day in the Life of Gerry and John . . .

Three days after the management group meeting in Gerry Avilla's office, Doug Bellingham had come to Gerry appealing for an adjustment to his portion of the budget. He felt that one particular element of the forecast was unfair: it called for him to sell more parts without a matching increase in inventory.

"See what I'm saying, Gerry? I believe we can sell as much as you and Barbara forecasted, but if you hold me to these inventory levels I'm afraid we'll be out of stock more often. Last year we lowered our back-order number by 7 percent, and this year by 3. So I feel like I've done a good job with turns, and would like to hold a percentage increase in inventory dollars as that matches the projected sales increase—for next year anyway."

"Doug, there's something wrong." Gerry slid a sheaf of papers over the desk to his parts manager and tapped it with his forefinger. "The folks at DAE have given us this report that shows the range of performances for all their dealers in the U.S., and to be honest we don't even make it halfway up the list on turnover ratios. I'm just asking for an improvement in overall turns from 5.5 you are hitting this year to a 5.9 next year." Gerry again tapped the papers Doug was trying to decipher and added, "Some of these dealers are hitting over six times turns. You can do it, man. I know you can."

"How, Gerry? Just show me how. Don't forget that nearly 40 percent of my sales are not on DAE products, so that distorts the figures. Some of these dealers sell nothing but DAE, so it's not a fair comparison."

"Just do your best, Doug. I tell you what: I'll split the difference with you. Raise the overall turns by just two-tenths of a percent. How's that? Then we can talk about doing a little better again the following year."

Chapter 15

Know Your Achilles' Heel

The ancient fable of Achilles usefully illustrates on a micro level the nature of all the challenges that have to do with the product or service weaknesses every business experiences. The mythical Greek warrior Achilles was invincible in battle, or so it seemed. He built a reputation that filled opponents with fear and trepidation, and then came the seemingly impossible; he was injured on his vulnerable heel and he was vanquished.

This story comes with an explanation for the hero's ultimate demise; as a newborn baby, Achilles' mother dunked him in "holy fire" to make him invincible. The problem is that the mother had to hold the baby by the heel as she dipped him in the fire, and that left a small part of him unprotected. The poisonous arrow of his conqueror, Paris, struck Achilles in the heel, leading to his death.

These days we refer to a personal weakness or a product weakness as our "Achilles' Heel." Unlike the fable, the weakness of any manufactured product is often obscure or uncertain simply because products get used in variable ways by people who can be careless or negligent—and in conditions that fluctuate. A simple product can conceivably be made totally reliable for all circumstances, but a complex one must face multiple usage uncertainties.

Illustration

In recent history in the automotive industry, massive recalls created quite a stir. Millions of Toyota and Lexus automobiles were recalled in 2011 due to reported problems of unexplained acceleration, in some cases causing accidents and even death. But there are constant recalls of products in many industries, though usually receiving less attention in the media than that example. Anyone who manufactures anything faces the challenge of deciding how perfect their products should be. Total perfection is hardly ever possible, or certainly not cost-effective, and yet some product types demand higher standards than others. To state the obvious, with any product involved in passenger transportation, the standards must be higher than for, say, a TV. The parameters for assessing a tolerable level of failures, or even an acceptable level of warranty claims, vary widely from industry to industry and are particularly difficult to deal with when third-party liabilities are also involved. And of course there's the issue of price variability. For each level of price there's a different marketplace expectation, a different level of tolerance for imperfection. If one buys an expensive item, the expectations for quality are high.

The previously mentioned spate of failures in certain automobiles illustrates the potential consequences of certain kinds of product weakness: huge expense, loss of consumer confidence. How does a thing like this happen?

All manufacturers need to establish a threshold of acceptable failure above which they take immediate recall action. In the heavy construction machinery industry, where I spent many years, we had a virtually industry-wide maximum failure rate (expressed as a percentage of revenues from the sales of machines) of 2.5 percent spent on warranty repairs. Any higher expenditure would indicate a manufacturing flaw on the product in question that needed to be corrected. As I said before, perfection is not possible—and heavy machinery routinely works in rugged conditions, but this number was purely arbitrary. Why not 2 percent? Why not 4 percent? And are there better ways to determine a need for revision or redesign? Furthermore, doesn't such an arbitrary measure encourage the denial of warranty claims by employees anxious to meet imposed profit goals and other targets? Even bonuses might figure into such decisions—you can see how.

Automobile manufacturers, as most people know, outsource a high percentage of their manufacturing to other companies. Several major suppliers of parts and components sell similar (sometimes identical) products to competing auto manufacturers. This certainly makes for cost containment synergies, but it also makes quality control and information flows between stakeholders alarmingly difficult. Remember, though, that the sole responsibility for failures rests on the shoulders of the company whose name is on the finished product.

Dealers can be involved, and can be helpful or not, further complicating the issue. So what can and should be done?

I insist that such questions and the difficulty in coming up with answers are the reasons a winning culture must be built, maintained, and sustained. The complete and enthusiastic involvement of each employee at every level in the processes of assured quality is the key. High-quality products come from a quality organization, not the other way around. Only if and when people are fully engaged in their work, fully understanding the mission, and fully understanding their roles and responsibilities and are rewarded for full engagement, are they likely to bring inevitable product weaknesses to the surface before failures rise to damaging levels. No employee should be happy to report a weakness, but they should also not be afraid to do so. Budget pressures, turf battles, along with petty individual differences and jealousies should not stand in the way of product weakness exposure, or the entire organization suffers. There is no room for the Persian messenger problem in the modern organization.

The Persian Messenger Syndrome: In Ancient Persia, so goes the legend, the King would cut off the head of anyone who brought him bad news. He wanted only good news, and this policy assured him he would get his wish.

Success—as measured by marketplace acceptance—often breeds complacency. All organizations must be aware of this threat, if people are afraid to deliver bad news. Head it off by showing trust and you'll sustain highly alert and proud human teams, eager to maintain the highest standards. But if the threat of lawsuits or of government intervention are the bases on which product redesign is triggered, then things have gone too far. Make certain—using all the approaches and guidelines in this book—that all your employees are alert to ways in which you can prevent or minimize problems proactively. Reward appropriate behaviors that do exactly that. You cannot avoid all product failures, of course, but you'll minimize the negative effects if you do these things on a continuing basis—even when you are very successful (perhaps especially then).

A Day in the Life of Gerry and John . . .

The specific Achilles' Heel of any one business, any one product, or even a whole product line has to be exposed and confronted in a real situation based on experience. Therefore no scenario has been developed for this chapter. Gerry and John have already demonstrated a few organizational weaknesses, plus some strengths on which they could build. They seem not to be terribly focused on building a winning culture, as defined in these pages, and at times have been rather closed-minded. But this will be further discussed in the end of the book summation. We are not in a position to deal with their product weaknesses. Whatever they might be, they should be acknowledged widely across their organization so that they can deal with them without pretense. This eliminates dishonesty in stressing other benefits related to unique features, instead of facing and fixing the problem.

Chapter 16

Quality: What and How

Remember that quality products and processes emerge from quality organizations, not the other way around. In American manufacturing circles more than four decades ago, the realization emerged that quality products come from attention to things other than the manufacturing standards themselves. Management scholars, and perhaps most business leaders, will tell you that W. Edwards Deming—in the 1950s—largely led this revelation, at first in Japan and then in American industry. Actually, with all due respect to Deming, I feel that he rode the wave, rather than drove it. How can that be?

Let me refresh the reader's memory by summarizing Deming's 14 key points (Deming, 1986):

- ❖ Create constancy of purpose toward improvement of product and service.

- ❖ Adopt the new philosophy of leadership for change.

- ❖ Cease dependence on inspection to achieve quality.

- ❖ End the practice of buying based on price. Instead, minimize total cost.

- ❖ Improve the system of production constantly and constantly decrease costs.

- ❖ Institute training on the job.

- ❖ Remember, the aim of supervision should be to help people do a better job.

- ❖ Drive out fear, so that everyone may work effectively for the company.

- ❖ Break down barriers between departments. All employees must work as a team.

- ❖ Eliminate slogans and targets exhorting zero defects and high productivity.

- ❖ Eliminate work standards (quotas) and MBO. Substitute leadership.

- ❖ Remove barriers that rob the hourly worker of his right to pride in workmanship.

❖ Institute a vigorous program of education and self-improvement.

❖ Put everybody in the company to work to accomplish the transformation.

I have edited these 14 points and in doing so, may have demeaned Deming's intentions, but even as modified, the above tabulation should clearly show what he had in mind: *A change of culture.*

But Deming was not the originator of this approach to the notion of an enriched culture and its role in delivering quality products and services. Beginning in the 1920s (see the landmark studies done at the Hawthorne plant of General Electric Co., originally documented by Roethlisberger and Dixon in *Management and the Worker*), the newly emerging business schools across America slowly produced a revolution in thinking about the workplace and about the workers, but almost exclusively this change was heeded only in academe. Businesses themselves did not pay much attention to this new theory of organization—not for a long time—so Deming found a haven for these ideals in Japan. There were two powerful reasons for this: First, by the end of World War II, Japanese industry had been completely decimated, so a ground-up renovation of some sort was needed and welcomed. Secondly, the Japanese psyche was better suited to the notion of teamwork and cohesion. Sociologists have partly explained this, using the notion of homogeneity of the culture—the inevitable reality of a small island nation. By comparison, American culture was probably the most heterogeneous in the world and the health of its industrial system at the time was robust. Individualism thrived here, in part because of our vast land, the existence of property rights, and so on, but also because it was inculcated into our psyche and it was built into our Constitution between the lines.

Changing a culture significantly—any culture—is extremely difficult. It also must be done in ways that reflect the current circumstances and existing conditions, and allowed to evolve rather than abruptly change. Real change needs powerful motivation, and a great deal of patience. Offering 14 points to guide such change is not much different from doing what Deming himself (in item 10) urged us to avoid, in fact: slogans and exhortations. Permanent change involves much risk-taking, sincere trust-building, and more than anything else, a willingness to accept glacial progress. Not an easy collection of attributes and methodologies, especially when facing the ravages of competition and the need to show productivity improvement and profits now.

So if you are in a position that seems to demand a change of culture in your organization, what can be done and how can it be brought about?

The first step—really just a precondition—is the most critical and foundational of all; make sure that everyone in the organization, especially all those in leadership positions, buys in to both the need for said change, and for the desired outcomes. This must be confronted openly, and in explicit terms. There's little value in saying something catchy, slogan-like, such as "A Commitment to Quality," which one organization I am familiar with developed as their guiding philosophy. That was as effective as making a new year's resolution, and we all know how that turns out most of the time. There's initial excitement and focus, but it fades rapidly.

This precondition is extremely difficult for one powerful reason: Some people will go along to get along, paying lip service only. Others may be defiant, just for the hell of it. So if you are an agent of change in your organization, first make a thorough assessment of your current position in all its complexities, and discuss that assessment widely and often. You should seek input from many, and be willing to accept different ideas from others. When you have reached a genuine consensus, you must get everyone enthused about a clear set of stated desirable outcomes and provide a timeline that everyone can embrace. There's absolutely no sense going ahead without this consensus. And by the way, if you set a timeline any less than two or three years to bring about significant levels of change, you are deluding yourself.

Then, and only then, are you ready to start the difficult job of creating a winning culture, while paying attention to and applying every suggestion in this book consistently. Yes, it is that important— and that demanding.

A Day in the Life of Gerry and John...

One day, John arrived at the office early and found Gerry up on a stepladder, attaching a huge banner high on the wall in the lobby.

"Ah, you're here, John. Grab the other end of this banner and climb that other stepladder with it. You'll see what it is when it's in place, but it's a surprise—for you and for everyone else. You'll see nails in the paneling up there, and there are grommet holes in the banner." The rest of the staff had not yet arrived.

They finished hanging the banner, a bright yellow sheet of plastic some 20 feet long, and John climbed down to take a look. It said:

"OUR CUSTOMERS ARE OUR #1 CONCERN!" in letters a full 15 inches high.

"What do you think?" Gerry asked.

"I think…well, it certainly is eye-catching, Gerry. And I like the sentiment. Catchy slogan!"

"I have another one just like it in the service shop, and a smaller one above the parts counter. Sets for the two branches as well. And I'm going to put that same slogan on all our advertising from now on. What about that?"

John liked the banners, though he was not quite sure what they would do for the company. But he went along, saying, "Nice job, Gerry. If you give the other banners to me I'll see to it that they'll get installed."

Chapter 17

Flexibility and Constraint

There are certainly many great examples of tyrannical leaders and bosses who get results. In the sports world, a figure such as football coach Vince Lombardi deserves immortal recognition. He produced a winning culture for years with the Green Bay Packers, mostly by being unwavering in his acceptance of anything less than perfection. Interestingly enough, he parlayed his successes to the business world, delivering motivational speeches to corporations based largely on one central tenet: *commitment*.

Yes, Vince, but how? That's the question.

In the modern age of business, in which there are realities quite different from those of a few decades back and certainly different from the relatively limited sphere of sports, people who work for you have less tolerance for heavy-handed treatment. Don't get me wrong; leaders can never afford to create the impression that they are without a firm hold on the reins. In fact, that aspect of your role has not changed, but you must be willing to listen to and learn from all the people on your payroll.

In American business, as opposed to businesses in Japan and other Asian countries, people tend to be promoted rapidly and vertically. Seldom, in this impatient era, will an employee ask for a lateral move to broaden their experience and exposure. For this reason, a manager cannot typically rely exclusively on the broad experiences of one or two key people. Chances are that there will have been a high degree of specialization in their backgrounds (and your own). So take the risk of seeking input, ideas, and commentary from a wide variety of employees, and here's the hard part; be flexible enough to heed their input. But do not allow yourself to be seen as lacking leadership strength. The balance between these constructs is challenging and yet critical to your success in building a winning culture.

A Day in the Life of Gerry and John . . .

"John, I don't want you to take offense," Gerry Avilla said, "but I don't think you have been paying attention to the used equipment advertisements we place every week. Look at this one, for instance. We sold that used DAE-533 two weeks ago, and this one too. Surely these listings should be more up to date than that."

John sighed. "Gerry, there's a good reason for this. Actually, two: If a customer calls about the machine we have found someone who's in the market. I can possibly turn the prospect toward a new machine, or toward a used machine we do have in stock."

"I get that. But I want to be sure that we don't advertise what we don't have for sale. It's an honesty thing, I guess. What's the other reason?"

"What? Oh, just that right now we don't have a lot of used inventory. With the slowdown we have been able to sell used items pretty fast. If we show a full list, people are more inclined to come in and take a look. It pays off, Gerry."

"Well, I still don't like it. Smacks of bait-and-switch. So keep it down to a minimum, will you? Humor me."

Chapter 18

Growth Traps

A strategic growth opportunity arises. Sounds great, right? But be fully aware of its price tag. Businesses of every size and type seek to grow—that is axiomatic. And although in some circumstances stagnation in size can be a healthy alternative, striving for growth is as natural as the survival instinct itself. There are several ways in which growth can be achieved, of course, so as a reminder I'll list the main ones here:

- ❖ growth from territorial expansion

- ❖ growth from improved market penetration

- ❖ growth from expanded products or services

❖ growth concomitant with market expansion or conversion

❖ growth from price increases (inflation).

The first two of these ways to grow are dependent on being able to literally take business away from competitors. The third could involve such "stealing" also, or it could be that the new products and services awaken a need or desire in an existing or untapped customer base. The fourth growth modality may not require a strategic choice or change, but simply relies on what is often called "windfall." The fifth is really a false growth, though it is often financially enriching to some degree simply because we end up paying off debt with devalued money. Even as price increases occur (in an inflationary environment, for example), business leaders must remain alert to the threat that their customers will seek alternative products and services (or seek alternative ways of fulfilling their needs) and you must find ways to obviate or offset this tendency.

Every business must come to a good understanding of exactly what makes their particular line of products and services of interest to potential customers. Earlier, I used the rather corny but appropriate example of an electric drill. No one (other than a few Tim-the-Tool-Man-Taylor types) buys an electric drill because they want to own the drill itself. Instead, people want what the drill will do for them: Reduce labor and time in drilling holes. So be sure that all your people have as complete a grasp as possible on what benefits your business provides for your customers in real terms.

And by the way, while on this subject, be sure that the designers and manufacturers of your "drill" never lose sight of why people buy drills, or whatever it is you make and sell. And also make sure they develop a good understanding of product life cycles. Virtually any product is doomed to be replaced by something better or perhaps cheaper. Anticipate the day, and plan for it carefully.

Armed with this critical understanding of what needs and wants you have the potential to satisfy, you are then in good position to answer with a crucial question about your growth plan: What is the marginal cost of adding customers to your client base? I mean the immediate or near-term cost of adding each new client, but also the long-term follow-on costs of every kind. Let me explain with a common example.

A blind and obsessive effort to grow a business often induces management to offer special incentives for attracting new customers; we see this all the time, in virtually every industry. Such incentives can indeed produce short-term results, but frequently the longer-term consequences and costs are overlooked or minimized. Incentives are essentially price reductions, so they inevitably reduce profits and add to expenses such as sales commissions. These costs can be offset by reducing inventories and all that such reductions entail, and perhaps some economies of scale enter the equation, but there's often a more insidious cost. If you offer new customers a special deal, what about existing customers who may have been loyal for years? How do you think they feel about your gift to new customers for which they themselves do not qualify? Furthermore, how can you know that your surge in current sales, spurred by an incentive program, did not merely accelerate buying activity at the expense of a future sales lag?

Illustration

This may surprise you, but if you check the data on what happened in the U.S. automobile industry during the August/September 2009 "Cash for Clunkers" incentive program, you see evidence for my claims about incentives unwisely used. The auto industry was in a deep recession at the time, and this program did indeed accelerate sales, but after the program was over, dealers everywhere experienced serious declines in demand. Furthermore, although the cost of the program in this case was borne by the taxpayers, the reported sales gains came at an expense far greater than was justified by the net growth experienced.

So here's a tip for all managers and strategic planners: Be sure to do a careful analysis of the potential unintended consequences of the plans you develop to grow your business. If you do in fact foresee some downside consequences (such as the ones I have mentioned and others of a similar nature), do a thorough cost-benefit analysis before making the final decision.

The old saying that "a bird in the hand is worth two in the bush" has merit, but in some circumstances it may not apply. Sometimes the two birds yet to be taken can be well worth the wait, but the most important thing is to think things through carefully and thoroughly. One can never know all the unintended consequences of a particular growth initiative, but one thing is clear: You can be sure that growth of every kind comes at a price. Every choice you make in life does.

As Vince Lombardi was fond of saying: *Your character is built by the accumulated effects of all your personal choices.*

A Day in the Life of Gerry and John...

Gerry Avilla entered John Standish's office with a Cheshire Cat grin on his face and sat on the corner of John's desk.

"Okay, I'll bite," John said. "What's got you stoked?"

"You'll never guess."

John laughed. "You won the lottery?"

"Not quite…but it could be almost that good. I had a call from Jason Armitage, he's the DAE dealer up in San Louis Obispo. He wants out, is ready to retire apparently. Offered us the opportunity to buy him out and take on all his obligations. I haven't checked, but I think DAE would give us financing if they approve us for the expansion. So why wouldn't we go for it?"

John had been listening, eyes getting wider with each revelation. "Why not indeed? You said yes, right?"

"I said we'd talk about it. There's a lot to consider, John. Yes, it would add about 50 percent to our revenues, but at a substantial cost. Armitage values his business at a figure that makes me pause, but he may be flexible. Seems DAE has been pushing him to add a substantial addition to the facility…which is the main reason it's for sale. We'd have a much larger nut to crack if we take it on, and so we need to be cautious. We already have a pretty good thing going for us, and we can expect growth when the economy fully recovers. The additional headaches of management and control would multiply, of course…but it sure is nice to be flattered by the offer, and we will give it full consideration. Armitage wants to meet us up in San Louis Obispo tomorrow for lunch. I'll drive."

Chapter 19

Difference, Conflict, Competition

There were earlier references to business culture and the notion that organizational culture is quite different from the culture of ethnicity and race; yet the underlying challenges of both have powerful commonalities. They are all based on perceived or real **differences**.

Oddly, perhaps, the virtually inevitable existence of differences between people does not call for different treatment; rather, they scream for **equal treatment**.

It is foolish to assume that all people who share common ancestry have the same values, the same desires, the same proclivities, or anything else of significance. It would be very pleasant in the world if everyone were to be judged solely on their individual traits, strengths, weaknesses, and behaviors, but sadly there remains a tendency for some people to stereotype. Though such tendencies linger—and they are less onerous than once was the case—to the degree that they exist at all they must not be ignored, as they are not only onerous from a humanitarian point of view, but they also pose a serious threat to building cohesion in your organization. Racism is a nasty word for an even nastier weakness—or fault—and although you, as a leader, can do little about the petty hatreds that lurk in the hearts of some people, you can do two powerful things to minimize the impact of such. First, go out of your way to overtly show the opposite sentiment, and second, make it clear that you will not accept the manifestation of any form of difference-based hatred or prejudice under any circumstances or by anyone, regardless of rank or stature.

The foregoing paragraph is simply a cautionary note about the most dangerous and noxious aspects of cultural clashes: the potential for conflict based solely on racial or ethnic differences. But differences of many kinds exist between people:

- ❖ age differences

- ❖ education level

- ❖ gender

- ❖ experience

- ❖ personality

- ❖ intelligence

- ❖ aptitude

- ❖ beliefs/religion

- ❖ health and fitness

- ❖ appearance

- ❖ maturity level.

And there are more, with many different dimensions of each difference. So this makes things too complicated for a concise book, therefore there isn't comprehensive advice on how to deal with conflicts that arise. Instead, I urge you to confront all but the most trivial forms of conflict that arise by applying just three simple but weighty principles of conflict resolution:

- ❖ Confront the situation openly with all parties together, inviting full disclosure.

- ❖ Treat each party equally, with respect and dignity.

- ❖ Bring focus on the superordinate goals.

I should point out that no attempt to deal with conflict resolution will be helpful unless you have conscientiously applied all the suggestions contained in this book. The reason for this is that you must have earned **trust**.

Furthermore, you can be sure there will be no willingness to refocus on the superordinate goals unless all parties have "signed on" and have committed to those goals. This will have come about only if you have delegated heavily but appropriately and have openly allowed goal-sharing, budgeting, and decision making at the lowest level possible.

This is the essential message of my book, and the good news is that if you have built a winning culture by following the guidelines, then the number of petty conflicts will have declined anyway, and the **superordinate** goals will prevail, encouraging cooperation and compromise to emerge.

Two Contrasting Illustrations

The government of the United States has been divided by conflict for many decades. We have a two-party system made up of Democrats and Republicans, and the bickering and rancor between them seems to have intensified to the point often described as deadlock. One would think that the general welfare of the Union and with the United States Constitution as our mission statement, cooperation and compromise would be the order of the day. But it isn't. And the reason is becoming clearer to me every day (I am a naturalized American citizen, with experience as a citizen in three countries); our two political parties do not share the same vision for America. Most Republicans wish to hold on to their interpretation of the original intent of the framers of the constitution, with a federalist system, strong states' rights, and a weak central government involved in as few of the citizens' lives as possible.

Most Democrats, or at least the "progressives" among them, by contrast, seem anxious to change the country in what they perceive to be a positive direction, by having the central government attempt to unify and control the activities of the people across all states, with equal outcomes for all as a central theme and a driving force.

Social scientist and author Thomas Sowell calls this impasse *A Conflict of Visions*, and he is right. For conflict to fade and progress to exist, a unified vision (superordinate goals) is the vital first step. Is such a thing possible in a land as diverse and as vast as the United States? I don't know, but I suspect that extraordinary leadership might give it a fighting chance.

My second illustration involves professional sports. Ever wonder what it would be like to play on a big-league team? Pick a sport. One of the major potential sources of conflict is salary difference. Top name stars get 20 to 30 times the money an average player makes. Would you tolerate that differential, when you see your contribution to the team as not all that much different from that of the team hotshots? But most players do accept it, and for a very good reason: They want to be a part of a winning team (a winning culture). The superordinate goals for the team are simple, clear, and well-understood by everyone. A championship, achieved one win at a time! Conflicts between professional athletes do occur, of course, and the source is usually something quite trivial by comparison: differences of another kind.

So let me repeat: Make sure the superordinate goals (your mission) are clear, evident, openly discussed, and fervently sought after by everyone on board. It will make your organization shine, so long as all the other pieces are in place. You will have a winning culture.

I need to add a few words about internal competition, and another aspect of conflict. The distinction between these concepts is important. Using sports as an example again, the game of golf is a form of perfect competition. Some go so far as to say that when playing golf you are merely pitting yourself against the course itself, and the challenges it presents. But try telling that to two professional golfers, tied for the lead at five under par in the final round, with millions watching on TV and a big paycheck difference between first place and second.

But the competition and the rules of the game as well as the traditions of etiquette do not allow one player to do anything directly to impede the success of the other. **Pure competition!**

In most other sports—team or individual—one player not only has to strive for perfection of his own game, but deliberately can and should use a strategy or tactic that impedes the other player. This is best exemplified in boxing. One fighter actually wishes to hurt the other with every punch, and ultimately to knock him unconscious. **Pure conflict!**

Competition then is healthy, and in sports it's…well, expected; but conflict in the workplace that does not necessarily lead to dysfunction can also be healthy. In fact, at modest levels and in certain circumstances it can be motivational. Good sports figures will tell you they would rather play against a good team than a weak one. They rise to the occasion, and victory is sweeter.

No, you're not playing a sport. But my point applies nevertheless. Some modest levels of conflict can be useful, so be prudent. No one can (or should) eliminate all difference-based conflict anyway, so let some of it work in your favor. With experience, you'll come to a fuller understanding of when and when not to intervene.

Chapter 20

Issues and Your Environment

As 17th-century poet John Donne wrote, "No man is an island, entire of itself," and he was right. Each of us as individuals, and each organizational collective, has a wide variety of interfaces and interdependencies. Your business is going to be affected by changes in your environment, changes in the law, and changes in social and behavioral patterns. There is every reason, therefore, for you and all your people to stay tuned to your environment and evaluate the available information it is constantly sending you. Sometimes the messages are difficult to interpret, but they are always there.

While very large organizations can afford to have a specialist (blue sky thinker, perhaps?) whose job it is to do this kind of evaluating and forecasting, most firms and organizations cannot. Therefore, you and many others should be encouraged to be constantly on the alert, reading newspapers, listening to community voices, checking legislative actions, and collectively discussing the potential short-term and long-term implications for your future. As part of this scanning process, the activities of your competitors should be monitored and evaluated. See this as part of your job. You will still get hit with surprises, but the overall benefits of remaining alert in this way can be lifesaving, or can at least keep you ahead of the pack.

Small organizations are generally more nimble than large ones, so they can adapt more readily and change courses as needed. But even a small boat captain needs to keep a sharp eye out for logs and rocks in the water. Furthermore, some businesses have a position in the marketplace based largely on followership rather than leadership—and there's no point in attempting to change a winning strategy. But just be aware: aware of who and what you are, what makes you successful, and what you do well. Do not depart from a winning pathway unless there's good reason.

Remember, the environment in which you operate is changing; I guarantee it. Only you can decide how the change affects you and your future. And you cannot, must not, take in and evaluate the inflow of information on your own. Share the burden with others you trust, and discuss it all frequently. This, as much as any other factor, is why I have stressed allowing all people within your organization to participate fully in the decision processes—to a level that matches their experience, ability, and commitment.

A Final Word

Much of the foregoing has to do with encouraging people at every level of your organization to grow, to participate, to share decision making, and to make heavy commitments—and also about why this is so important. I have focused this book substantially on these concepts because such are the keys to a winning culture. Yet, there's a caveat.

Some people just want a job. They just want to get along and go along, are content to be led, even to be told what to do and how to do it. Such people are *not* the "keys" I mention at the start of this book. They may have value, nevertheless, and be worthwhile employees, but they are not the ones I have written about herein.

Given that reality, it is up to you to decide whether having such people on board is acceptable in your particular set of circumstances. If it is, okay, but how many of them and in what kind of positions?

Every organization is unique, and many have great success without being especially dynamic, creative, or forward-thinking. Truth to tell, if you are in such a situation you will probably not have purchased this book, so let me address you as one who is anxious to be progressive, eager to create a winning culture.

Do not place a complacent person, or a person who does not want to grow and improve their own status, in a position of leadership or in positions that have significant influence over others. *Never.*

Do not allow too many complacent people to remain on your payroll. There's no hard and fast rule or ratio for this, but certainly more than one or two such people in close proximity to others more aggressive—no matter how pleasant or enjoyable they may be—can be a significant deterrent in your efforts to build a winning culture, because they tend to offset the enthusiasm of others.

But do not automatically take *apparent* complacency as an unwillingness to grow and take on responsibility. A lack of self-confidence often presents itself as complacency, so be patient with such a person and give them ample time to come around. Give them support, encourage them, mentor them, and you may see a change of attitude take place. This is especially likely when others around them are building enthusiasm in desirable ways.

Most businesses, I have found, and indeed most organizations of every kind, are badly managed in ways that are relatively easy to identify (especially after you read this book). The examples and the end-of-chapter exercises are designed to get you to recognize the several ways in which your personal (on the job) activities, attitudes, and responses to others affect the overall process of your organization. There are no magic bullets that apply to all situations, but the guidelines and suggestions contained herein are reliable and time-tested ways to build and sustain a winning culture. Apply them consistently, persistently, and fairly and you will see sparkling results. You will see the emergence of a winning culture.

But do not walk on eggshells. You will make mistakes, drop the ball, fail to do the right thing from time to time; but people are not so fragile that errors of the sort dealt with in this book will destroy your efforts to build a winning culture. And with practice and experience, all the while being as conscientious as you can be, you will continue to get better.

In addition, you will enjoy the process, the sense of accomplishment, and the satisfaction that comes when you change things according to a plan, and change them for the betterment of everyone involved. A winning culture is fun to be a part of, always!

It is never too late to get started. Stick with the program. You'll be glad you did.

Appendix

About the "Day in the Life" Exercises

Some readers will have made notes on the end-of-chapter exercises and others will perhaps not have done so. If you did, or even if you didn't but still read the scenarios anyway, the following discussion may help you realize the various ways the fictitious company described could improve their chances of building and sustaining a winning culture, even though most of the key points made in the book are not directly represented in the scenarios.

It should have become obvious to readers that although the various subjects and chapter materials have been dealt with separately—for convenience and clarity of message—they often interrelate in the real world of organizational life. And, it must be said, in everyday life the various issues become muddled, less obvious, and are therefore more difficult to confront and correct.

The following analysis picks out only the items worth noting as the most powerful influencers of the organization's culture.

A Day in the Life of Gerry and John...

Chapter 1 The Hiring Scenario

John Standish made several cardinal errors in his failure to adequately prepare for his interview of an applicant for the open sales position. Yes, unforeseen circumstances can make life difficult, and it is easy in a busy day to forget commitments made that serve to impair preparations. He would have been better off if he had asked the candidate to reschedule, rather than go forward with a sloppy and damaging interview. He did, in fact, consider canceling the appointment with his contractor, and his wife reminded him there was a time constraint.

Let's tabulate John's most egregious errors:

❖ He forgot obligations that prevented his appropriate preparation.

❖ He missed the opportunity to ask the candidate to reschedule.

❖ Because of poor personal discipline, he showed up late.

❖ He failed to put the candidate at ease with friendly chatter.

❖ He even forgot the candidate's name, and called him by the wrong name.

Not a great start in an important process, because he should see this as an opportunity to start building confidence in the potential employee. How would you perceive this organization if you were the candidate and had been treated in this manner?

Chapter 2 The Training Scenario

In this scenario, John Standish showed four key weaknesses:

- ❖ He demonstrated an anxious concern about call-report bureaucracy.

- ❖ He rejected peer training for the new sales representative.

- ❖ He responded negatively to Sergio's criticism about lack of encouragement.

- ❖ He displayed a poor attitude toward the opportunity to interview the office manager.

Call reports can be of immense value to a sales manager, for all sorts of reasons. But John should either communicate what those values are in precise terms or be more flexible. The best sales call report is, of course, a customer order. Salespeople should be measured and evaluated on results and profit contribution; all else is gingerbread. Other paperwork can be of value in targeting and promotion efforts, but if it is administered with a heavy hand it is discouraging, and can be demotivating.

Peer training is fraught with dangers, of course, as the bad habits of one person can be learned by the other. But it is the sales manager's job to see that the new hire in this case gets a broad exposure to the territorial peculiarities and challenges, to the methods and approaches of the most successful salesmen, and then gets the sales manager's overall guidance as well. To resist allowing the new candidate to benefit from peer training (not the least of which is a speedy assimilation onto the team) is a show of immaturity in John Standish, and perhaps even a level of insecurity.

As for the plea by Sergio for more encouragement from his boss, Standish showed a lack of understanding when he said to Gerry Avilla he thought Sergio should be motivated and encouraged by the money he makes, and should not expect to be coddled. This is a blatant disregard for the fact that everyone appreciates recognition; though individuals vary in how important this is to them. A good manager knows the different needs of the people he is responsible for, and in no way is this coddling.

Finally, Standish's reluctance to meet with a potential candidate for the manager's job is disturbing to say the least. We learn later that he did in fact meet with her, but as a partner in the business he should be keenly interested in the hiring of anyone, and especially someone in a key position. Perhaps a show of insecurity again?

Chapter 3 Meetings

John Standish's insecurities are also on display in this scenario. He is preparing for a sales meeting, and although he is wise enough to reject the motivational speaker who has a canned and dated approach to motivating salespeople, he demonstrates four classic errors, all of which could well relate to insecurities of his own, but should have been confronted by Gerry Avilla also:

- ❖ There's no indication of what the purpose of the meeting is.

- ❖ Standish is focusing again on bureaucratic concerns and call reports.

- ❖ The agenda is not driven by real needs and concerns.

- ❖ Standish seeks no input from the meeting participants.

I mention the complicity of Gerry Avilla because, as his partner and supervisor, he should have trained his sales manager well enough that these problems would not exist. A meeting with these flaws in planning is doomed to fail because the attendees will get the message that their boss sees them as his subordinates more than collaborators in a unified cohesive effort. Even the most charismatic of leaders needs enthusiastic support from followers, and from what we have learned thus far, John Standish is not by any means a compelling figure.

Chapter 4 Office Relationships

Gerry Avilla is the errant party in the chapter 4 scenario. He blatantly invites the credit and collections guy, Jake, to dinner and a hockey game, and it is evident that he has done this on prior occasions. An even-handed approach is called for in the disposition of such perks, and at least others should be given the opportunity to decline the invitation. This kind of favoritism breeds resentment that often leads to rumor-mongering. The two office personnel may not be interested in going to a hockey game themselves, but their chatter about Gerry's wife and her fancy car are sure signs that they hold a grudge that is complex and widely based—though they may not actually be aware of the fact.

Chapter 5 Who Gets the Credit?

John Standish's insecurity is on display again. His insistence on taking credit for closing the sale on a large deal is quite pathetic. Even if Lance (the sales rep on the deal) did very little in the final phase of the close, a mature sales manager would take the opportunity to cede him credit to some degree, rather than lamely saying "Lance didn't have much to do with it."

Gerry Avilla should also have taken this opportunity to correct John's attitude a little. If Standish really has a sales representative unable to close the deal without a great deal of assistance, Gerry should have focused on that point and asked what could be done to strengthen Lance's sales ability. At this point, Gerry should be seeking ways to strengthen the overall team in such important ways. There's no harm celebrating a small victory the way these two did, but by the same token, these business owners need to be constantly striving for a consistent improvement in every aspect of what they do.

Chapter 6 Dealing With Underperformers

It seems as if Gerry's service manager (Jaime Alvarez) has already made up his mind that an underperforming mechanic should be terminated. The kind of failings the mechanic is demonstrating certainly would justify termination, but not without first exploring all the options for improvement, and imposing a timeline based on specific criteria for measuring progress. Gerry's nudge about "personal problems" shows that he instinctively knows this could be a factor, but when Jaime dismisses that approach with his "nursemaids" comment, Gerry lets it slide. One cannot help but conclude that Gerry has not properly trained his service manager, and is not showing strength in leadership by guiding the man with a firm hand. It is always possible in a situation like this that there's a personality clash between the mechanic and his direct supervisor. Such a possibility remains undisclosed because the right questions have not been asked by Gerry.

Chapter 7 Orchestration

A customer inconvenienced, or worse—caused unnecessary cost—is a customer unlikely to remain faithful. The error in the parts department involves sloppy handling of a back-ordered part that was supposed to be held on arrival for one customer but was in fact sold to another inadvertently. This is a system error compounded by a failure among people in the parts department to coordinate their efforts. Never mind that the part in question is one for which the company usually sees little demand. In fact, if that were not the case, the problem would not have occurred, as the part would have been on the shelf initially. Never mind that the original order was lost in shipment—such things do happen. A careful coordination of efforts among the employees involved would have prevented this serious problem. Gerry Avilla did the right thing in correcting the problem, but at high cost. Preventing problems is, or should be, the department manager's prime responsibility, not that of the General Manager. That responsibility should include focused training of all the people under his influence. Fixing problems after the fact is something to be avoided whenever possible.

Chapter 8 Cheerleading

Gerry is doing something wise and positive in gathering everyone together to announce the big sale. This is a form of cheerleading that encourages employees and makes them feel good about the way things are going—provided it is handled correctly. We do not get to see exactly what Gerry says to the gathering, but if he makes a fuss over John Standish himself (who claimed primary responsibility for the sale) or even over the hapless salesman, Lance, it will be an opportunity wasted. Instead, he should casually mention the names of these men but should applaud the efforts of the entire organization. And he should thank everyone. He should also make a few brief remarks about the future, the things yet to be accomplished. Then, after the gathering is over, he should ask John and Lance to step into his office and thank them personally for their efforts and explain why he had de-emphasized their role to the entire staff.

Chapter 9 Lower Cultural Boundaries

When Doug Bellingham asks for an opportunity for his people to participate in or at least attend a sales meeting, he is demonstrating a keen insight. Although the two departments operate independently most of the time and face their own unique challenges, it is important for the players in all departments to feel a sense of belonging, that their efforts are an important contribution to the success of the whole. To create and nurture such a sense of involvement and significance, sharing experiences is important and having cross-departmental attendance at meetings is just one way to accomplish this important goal.

But there's a catch: If John runs a top-down bureaucratically-centered meeting, the parts personnel in attendance will get little if any value from being involved. In fact, there is likely to be a negative effect. We hear Doug—after the meeting— telling John that his people enjoyed the meeting, and about one person going even further in expressing his enthusiasm, so maybe John ran a good, democratic, and purposeful meeting. But it is also possible that Doug's people simply reported what Doug wanted to hear. Hypocrisy exists in many forms in a dysfunctional organization.

Chapter 10 Matchups

Barbara King, the applicant for the office manager's job, has the *potential* to become an overqualified person in an important position. There is also another *possibility;* her timidity might turn out to be another form of mismatch, but these are the vagaries of hiring people, especially when those doing the hiring don't agree, or don't have a definite set of criteria for the position in question. Lack of preparation is again in evidence, and as always, one of the bad outcomes of a poorly prepared selection can indeed be a mismatch.

Even when precise criteria for hiring are worked out in advance, there's no guarantee a perfect match will be made, so levels of deviance from the ideal need to be discussed and evaluated. There's no evidence that Gerry and John have done anything like this kind of work. Again, the everyday job of meeting current challenges and putting out fires supplants careful planning of every kind. But this natural weakness must be overcome for a winning culture to have a chance.

Chapter 11 Trust...

There's nothing wrong with Gerry's idea of sharing ownership of the business with key people. But to bring up the possibility for one such person (a virtual outsider especially) before even broaching the subject with the one key person who is already an owner is a gigantic blunder. John shows his disappointment in a relatively mild manner, but most people would be extremely angry with Gerry over this. It is guaranteed to undermine trust between the two for a long time.

See also under chapter 13, in the last paragraph of the discussion about budgets imposed from the top, and how a lack of opportunity to provide important decision input is—or can be—a trust buster. Middle managers especially resent top-down budgeting and other forms of heavy-handed bureaucratic treatment. It makes them feel insignificant and it misses one of the best methods of building a trust level that must exist for a winning culture to flourish.

Chapter 12 Feature the Benefits

Ned Baxter tried hard to convince his customer that the tractor the man had been looking at was feature-rich, and he certainly sounded convinced of the importance of the items he mentioned. But he failed to show how those features would translate in customer benefits. That comfy operator's seat would perhaps prevent the operator from getting too tired to pay close attention to his work during a long day of plowing, for instance. But you get the picture.

John Standish seemed aware that Ned needed help, but he was prevented from stepping in—or was he? Whatever the phone call might have been, he should have asked for someone else to take the call and jumped in to help Ned.

More importantly, all of the salespeople should have been trained to feature the benefits in every sales presentation. This too represents a failing on the part of the sales manager.

Chapter 13 Budgeting Pitfalls

Ah, the dreaded imposed-from-the-top budget rears its ugly head. Well, belatedly, Gerry Avilla does ask for feedback from his managers on any problems with the budget, but the source of information on potentials for revenues and expense accounts should have included inputs from each of his department managers. They would get input wherever appropriate, including from their people. The GM then would have the prerogative of adjusting on the basis of his own analysis, but doing things the way Gerry did in this case is probably all too common. It represents a missed opportunity to build a winning, fully participative management team.

But there's another error disclosed in this brief scenario. Compounding the fact that Gerry has failed to seek input from lower organizational components to build the budget is the fact that he and the office manager have conspired in this effort. So this will (or could) be seen by the department managers as a form of favoritism. Yes, the new office manager has some special abilities with financial planning and accounting, but a budget is much more than figures on a piece of paper; it is an operational plan for guiding the activities of everyone on board. It is a reasonable assumption that such an alliance (GM and office manager) could severely hamper or undermine the much-needed trust essential in a winning culture.

Chapter 14 The Goal-Setting and Forecasting Scenario

Shared goal setting is an important way of maintaining high levels of commitment among employees at every level, but especially for key managers. This becomes even more critical when performance bonuses or other awards are attached to goal attainment. In this scenario, Doug (the parts manager) has a good argument in defense of his request for goal adjustment, but his boss should have been well aware of the mix of products the parts manager has to deal with before even thinking of imposing goals. Gerry's failure as a leader in this respect is potentially damaging because it undermines trust. Shared goal setting begins with mutual exploration of all the relevant variables at play...otherwise it can be transformed into a combative process.

Chapter 16 Quality

There's nothing inherently wrong with the banners Gerry Avilla obtained extolling the virtue of caring about customers. And certainly the expense in this case is minimal. The same can be said for adding a matching slogan to all their printed promotional materials—it can do little harm. But the best way to show customers that they're the company's "#1 Concern" is to deliver consistently good or excellent service. Imagine an awful marriage in which an abusive husband is always telling his battered wife he "loves her deeply." This is an extreme example, but actions always speak louder than words! Quality is as it becomes operationalized! Remember that Edward Deming said, "Eliminate slogans," but I would modify that to: Make sure that any slogan you use is matched by what you actually do.

Chapter 17 Flexibility and Constraint

In the assignment at the end of chapter 17, we see Gerry flexing his muscles unreasonably. John Standish has a valid reason for doing what he does, so accusing him of not "paying close attention…" is overbearing and inflexible. His insistence on "honesty" is undermined by his request to "keep it to a minimum." Honesty, but not complete honesty is the message.

But in addition to this we have seen a few examples of John Standish's management style in the prior scenarios, and in particular we have seen his own inflexibility over the issue of call reports. Salespeople are almost like independent contractors in many situations, and they need more autonomy than most people who work on site all the time. Because their activities are remote and off site, many sales managers in all kinds of industries insist on a system of call reports—and they can be useful, true, but they can also be seen as a thinly disguised policing method.

Frankly, with a sales force as small as John's, and with the total area of coverage so small—allowing frequent face-to-face contact with sales representatives and even more frequent phone contact—I would much rather see John ask each salesperson to keep him informed daily of what is going on in the territory with phone calls, and for less urgent communications, use email messages, or even text messages. This should ensure that, when needed, the sales manager can hop in his car and join up with a sales rep in need of help to close a deal pronto…or even to help develop a prospect. Such a method also ensures closer relationships, and that more timely actions are taken. More importantly, it is a less bureaucratic and heavy-handed method of staying in touch and dealing with issues as they arise.

If Standish can demonstrate that the call reports he relies upon can improve the marketing effort in some finite ways, then there may be good reason for insisting on adherence to his policy. If not, he should abandon it or de-emphasize it, and he should not be so quick to criticize reps who find it of little value.

Chapter 18 Growth Traps

How tempting it is for Gerry and John to buy the existing matching business and expand their territory, their revenues, and their potential profits. Such a move would challenge their management skills immensely, but more importantly it would come at a hefty price; one they should examine carefully before leaping into the expansion. A full cost-benefit analysis is called for, including the tangible as well as the intangible benefits and burdens. Many a small business grows its way into failure.

Faced with this kind of decision, the partners might consider taking another small step that could increase the likelihood of a winning culture developing: offering part (minority) ownership to the key personnel already on board and those they would acquire if they do buy the Armitage dealership. This would be especially important if they offer minority ownership to the lawyer, as Gerry proposed earlier.

Chapter 19 Difference, Conflict, Competition

Something to watch for whenever there is a merger or acquisition is the possibility of a culture clash. Dealing with all the challenges of the takeover itself is going to be difficult enough for Gerry and John without them having to handle any significant differences, resentments, or conflicts hidden beneath the surface and perhaps even aggravated by the takeover itself.

Too many companies purchase control of another strictly on the basis of financial analysis, and yet of equal importance are all the subtleties and dynamics of the human organization itself.

Chapter 20 Issues in the Environment

If the buyout does take place, Gerry and John will be newcomers in a major chunk of fresh territory, and yet they must quickly get their ear to the ground on all the external realities and issues that are peculiar to this new environment. If there are resentments lurking among employees and managers of the San Louis Obispo dealership, it could hamper their efforts to include the "locals" in evaluation of the external threats and opportunities presented. These are trying times (mergers and takeovers) for everyone involved. Tensions mount, uncertainties prevail, and differences are amplified.

Note: Some of the chapters in this book were based on articles originally published in *Why Not!* magazine. This business, economics, and social issues quarterly is now an Internet magazine (www.whynotmagazine.
com) and is a great source of tips and guidelines for executives and managers in any industry. I recommend it highly. I am just one of several highly
qualified people who write for *Why Not!* Give it a try—you'll find it a foun-
tain of useful information.

References

Barnes, A.K.(1994). *Management Maturity: Prerequisite to Total Quality Management*. Lanham, MD: University Press of America.

Blanchard, K., and S. Johnson. (1981). *The One Minute Manager*. New York: William Morrow.

Deaver, M.K. (2001). *A Different Drummer*. New York: HarperCollins.

Deming, W.E. (1986). *Out of the Crisis*. Cambridge, MA: MIT Press.

Peters, T.J., and R.H. Waterman, Jr. (1982). *In Search of Excellence*. New York: HarperCollins.

Roethlisberger, F.J., and W.J. Dickson. (1939). *Management and the Worker*. Cambridge, MA: Harvard University Press.

Sowell, T. (2007). *A Conflict of Visions: Ideological Origins of Political Struggles*. New York: Basic Books.

About the Author

A. Keith Barnes served as the S. V. Hunsaker Professor of Management at the University of Redlands in Southern California from 1984 to 1999, where he won awards for teaching and service. He authored the academic book *Management Maturity: Prerequisite to Total Quality Management* and more than 60 articles and monographs on a wide variety of business subjects. He holds a doctorate in Organizational Leadership and an MBA, both from Pepperdine University. His undergraduate work was completed in England (Mechanical Engineering) and in Canada (Psychology). Before becoming an academic, he was a senior executive with the J. I. Case Company, which was then a part of the Fortune 500 Company Tenneco, Inc.

A prolific writer, Barnes (pen name Arch Barnes) has published several novels in two genres, and using his full name he writes feature articles for an international magazine on a wide variety of topics in the realm of business, economics, and public policy. He has also served on three academic editorial boards and was editor of the Journal of

Applied Business Research from 1988-97. His biography has been listed in *Who's Who in American Education, Who's Who in Business and Finance, Who's Who in America,* and *Who's Who in the World.*

Index

Index